Family Food & Weekend Feasts

Family Food & Weekend Feasts

JANELLE BLOOM

Photography by Steve Brown

EBURY
PRESS

Contents

Words from a friend

From the moment I met Janelle Bloom, sparks were flying and a special friendship was formed. That was six years ago now – and 10 kilos ago too, for both of us! (Janelle's famous brownies from *Fast Fresh & Fabulous* have been a major contributor – but gosh they are good.)

This is book three in the series, and how beautiful it is. What I like about Janelle's books, Janelle's cooking, is that the recipes are easy to duplicate – foolproof even – because she's so willing to share her knowledge, secrets and tips. Her dishes are inexpensive, always delicious, and you'll feel a sense of pride when you serve them to your loved ones.

We are great mates, which means I have her on call 24/7. Janelle has received many a frantic phone call from me, day and night, seeking culinary help. Even if she's fast asleep when I call, she calmly refers me to a page or tip in one of her books – and then rolls over and goes straight back to sleep. She is a generous, giving friend.

I love Janelle and I am proud of her. I know you will love this book and you too will feel a little closer to Janelle as you create her food for your family, friends and, most importantly, yourself.

Happy cooking and creating – phone me if you need her number for help!

Peter Everett

Introduction

Good food should be a part of everyday life – and it always has been for me. I grew up in a family where my lunch box was packed for me most days, and the evening meal was about more than just the food – it was time to sit down together and talk. A tough day at school never seemed so bad when Mum was dishing up beautiful freshly cooked schnitzel, or when I could smell chocolate pudding baking in the oven. Food cooked with love has a way of delivering good memories that live on, and that's what this book is all about.

I sometimes spend whole days planning the meals I am going to cook for the week. Other weeks are not as well planned, but there is one constant – delicious home-cooked food every day. While I would love to be able to spend all day thinking and planning every meal, the pace of life most days is just way too busy – but I am never too busy to cook and I don't find cooking a chore. Why? No, not because I am good at it, but because the best way to keep yourself motivated and inspired night after night is to keep serving up new recipes. Try it, just one new recipe a week, even if it's a new salad or side dish.

I've split this book into three parts (which is kind of how my life is split): midweek meals for the family to enjoy; weekend feasts to inspire and delight; and food to share with your loved ones that will make entertaining pure pleasure. The main meals are fresh, colourful and absolutely delicious, with plenty of the nutrients vital for good health, and the sweets are to die for. All are created so that the ingredients are easy to find, the preparation requires very little fuss, and washing-up is kept to a minimum. My trademark tips are designed to make you feel as though I'm there holding your hand from start to finish.

Cooking for family and friends is the way I show them how much I love them. I hope as you cook from the pages that follow, you too will add a sprinkling of your love to every dish.

Happy days ahead,

Janelle

Ingredients

Asian sauces
When I need Asian sauces such as hoisin, plum or char sui, I use the Lee Kum Kee brand. They are authentic, well priced and available at many supermarkets and Asian grocery stores.

Breadcrumbs
When a recipe calls for 'soft' breadcrumbs, I mean that they should be homemade from stale bread. The crusts can be left on for savoury dishes but should be removed for sweet recipes.

Butter
I use regular salted butter unless otherwise specified. Margarine changes the flavour and texture of baked goods and I am not a fan.

Chocolate
I insist on good-quality chocolate, and almost always use dark Plaistowe from the baking aisle of the supermarket (now called Plaistowe premium dark real chocolate for cooking). I also use Plaistowe white and milk chocolate if a recipe calls for melting, but if the chocolate is to be chopped, your favourite brand from the confectionery aisle is the perfect choice.

Coconut milk and cream
I always use Ayam brand, though there are numerous authentic brands just as good. If you use another brand, the consistency may vary. Note that reduced-fat coconut milk or coconut cream curdles when heated.

Eggs
All the recipes in this book use standard-sized 59g eggs from the fridge, unless otherwise specified. My preference is for free-range organic.

Filo pastry
Don't be tempted to use any brand other than Antoniou, found in the fridge section of the supermarket. Though it has a shorter shelf life than the frozen sheets, pastry from the fridge is never stuck together when you open it.

Frozen berries
I love the Creative Gourmet brand for frozen berries and cherries. The quality never disappoints and they hold their shape when thawed.

Ginger
Fresh ginger root appears regularly throughout my books. If the skin is pale and papery thin there is no need to peel it – just scrub before use. If the skin is dark and feels dry, peel with a sharp knife before use.

Green onions
Green onion is the name I use for the bunches of long, thin green and white onions, harvested when the tops are green but before the bulb has started to mature. Other names for these bulbs include green shallots, shallots, spring onions or scallions.

Ice-cream
If a recipe calls for ice-cream to be softened and then re-frozen, I suggest Blue Ribbon brand, as it resets without forming icy crystals. If the ice-cream is to be served as a scoop on the side of a dish, buy the best you can afford, or make it yourself.

Icing sugar
There are two kinds of icing sugar available: pure icing sugar and icing sugar mixture. Pure icing sugar is white sugar that has been processed to a fine white powder; it sets firmer and can be quite lumpy in the

packet, which is why it must always be sifted. Icing sugar mixture has a small amount of cornflour added to keep it soft and lump-free. Where you can use either in recipe, I just say 'icing sugar', but where it really has to be pure, that's what I specify. (I personally prefer pure icing sugar in all cases, even though sieving out lumps can be time-consuming.)

Mascarpone

I like to use South Cape mascarpone because it doesn't curdle or separate as quickly as other brands when you stir it or add other ingredients.

Milk

I use full-fat milk for cooking in all my recipes. For some recipes you can substitute low-fat if you like (though I never would!), but remember that low-fat milk can curdle when it's boiled and the consistency of the final product will be different.

Olive oil

The olive oil brands available in the supermarket are fine for all-purpose everyday cooking. Generally the more you pay, the better the quality. Invest in a good-quality bottle of extra-virgin olive oil and use it for salad dressing, or to drizzle over food just before serving – you will notice the difference.

Parmesan

I always use a fresh block of parmesan cheese. When a recipe calls for it to be finely grated I use a microplane grater, otherwise a regular box grater will do.

Pasta

The secret to cooking pasta is to start with a good-quality durum wheat pasta and you can't go wrong. Make sure you boil a really large pan of water, as salty as the sea, and be kind on the environment by pouring the cooled water over the garden, not down the sink.

Puff pastry

Supermarket puff pastry sheets are a good stand-by, but I like to use the restaurant-quality puff pastry made by Carême. It's available from specialty stores in blocks and sheets, and well worth the extra expense. It's easier working with pastry sheets when they are still a little frozen.

Ricotta

I use quite a lot of ricotta throughout my books. It's always fresh ricotta from the deli, not the spreadable tub version. Remove any liquid from the container daily, as it causes fresh ricotta to sour quickly.

Salt & pepper

Sea salt flakes and freshly ground black pepper are what I use. The only time I use fine table salt is to produce crackling on pork rind or for seasoning and cleaning a wok.

Spices

Good-quality spices are an essential part of a well-stocked pantry. When you open a packet or jar you should be almost bowled over by the aroma. No aroma equals no flavour.

Sugar

The white sugar used throughout this book is everyday coarse sugar. Other coarse sugars, such as demarara or raw sugar, can be used, but when a recipe calls for caster sugar it is best not to use substitutes.

Vanilla

Vanilla is one of my favourite ingredients. I choose to use vanilla extract, vanilla paste or a vanilla bean, rather than vanilla essence. These have a far more intense and purer flavour, so you require only half as much. If you are using essence, you will need to use at least twice as much as my recipes state.

Vinegar

Whether it's balsamic, cider, red wine or any other variety, choosing a good-quality vinegar is paramount. Cheap supermarket vinegars can really spoil a dish.

Yoghurt

Greek yoghurt is another commonly used ingredient used throughout my books, and Farmers Union brand is my favourite. When cooking, don't be tempted to use reduced-fat options, as they will curdle.

Equipment

Baking paper, foil and kitchen wrap
Purchase the best you can afford. Cheaper options are a false economy, as you usually require twice as much.

Cake pans
Baking is a science, and therefore I leave nothing to chance. My recipes will always tell you the dimensions or the capacity of the pans I use. It is important to use a pan the same size and shape or very similar in order to be assured of success.

Cups & spoon measures
Make sure you have Australian Standard measuring cups and spoons. In Australia, a teaspoon is 5ml, and a tablespoon is 20ml. When measuring, ingredients should always be level.

Electric mixer
If you like baking, a benchtop electric mixer is a must-have appliance.

Heat-proof, microwave-safe cookware
Pyrex or similar is my choice for use in the microwave. I prefer cookware that is multi-functional, as cupboard space is at a premium in all kitchens.

Julienne peeler
The julienne peeler is well used in my kitchen when preparing carrots, cucumber, zucchini, green papaya and mango. These are way cheaper to buy at Asian grocery stores.

Cooking on the stove & in the oven

Oven temperature

As the majority of homes have fan-forced ovens these days, most of the recipes in this book give a fan-forced oven temperature. As a traditionalist, I bake with the fan off, so I have given both temperatures where applicable, but I find some recipes just don't live up to my expectations when cooked in a fan-forced oven. In these cases, only the no fan temperature is given.

Microwave ovens

Throughout my books you will see numerous references to using the microwave oven where it saves time and washing-up without compromising on results. All microwave ovens are preset to start at 'High' or 100%, power, so that's the level we tend to use the majority of the time, which is a mistake. It is often best to use an alternative setting. High = 100%; Medium-high = 70%; Medium = 50%; Medium-low or Defrost = 30%; Low = 10%.

Shallow-frying

When shallow-frying, it's important not to overcrowd the pan. Too much food too close together causes the temperature of the oil to drop, and the food will stew, rather than forming a beautiful golden crust. The food will also absorb more oil.

Deep-frying

Deep-fried foods should be enjoyed sparingly. Never fill a pan, fryer or wok over halfway. Check that the oil is hot enough by dipping a wooden chopstick or a wooden spoon handle in the centre of the pan. If small bubbles appear, the oil is ready. Cook in small batches, and allow the oil to reheat between batches. It is important to maintain a constant temperature.

Draining fried foods

When draining food that has been cooked in oil, I prefer to remove it to a wire rack over a tray lined with paper towel, for two reasons. First, the food can stick to the paper towel; second, the paper towel traps steam, softening the food's crisp surface. A wire rack can be popped into the oven to keep the food warm while you're cooking in batches, and the air circulating around the rack will keep the food crisp.

Family food

Time is the one thing most of us would like more of (besides money, of course). It seems the world is spinning faster every day. Our lives are so full we just don't have the time to plan the family meal like generations before us did. We still face the daily dilemma — 'What am I going to have for dinner?' — but on a weeknight, food has to be fast, nutritious and fuss-free.

Midweek meals

With limited time to plan and shop on weekdays, we find ourselves cooking the same meals over and over again. This chapter is dedicated to expanding your weeknight repertoire — whether it's dressing up barbecue lamb chops with a delicious lemon curd dressing, experimenting with sensational new salads and side dishes, or adding a dollop of homemade relish or chutney when serving up sausages. I urge you just to try one new recipe each week — the reward of empty dinner plates and eternal gratitude awaits!

Roasted carrot & parsnip soup

I have used vegetable stock to keep this recipe vegetarian. Make sure it's good vegetable stock. Feel free to use chicken stock if you prefer.

Serves 4

400g (3 small) parsnips, peeled, trimmed, roughly chopped ♥

750g (4 large) carrots, peeled, trimmed, roughly chopped

1 tablespoon honey

2 tablespoons olive oil

1 teaspoon freshly grated nutmeg

5-6 cups vegetable stock

hot buttered toast, to serve

♥ Cut larger parsnips down the centre. If you see a woody core, trim it out with a sharp knife.

1 Preheat the oven to 180°C fan-forced. Combine the parsnip and carrot in a lightly greased roasting pan. Microwave the honey in a heat-proof bowl for 20 seconds on High/100%. Drizzle the honey and oil over the vegetables. Sprinkle with nutmeg and season with salt and pepper, then toss to coat. Roast for 30–40 minutes, or until tender.

2 Pour 5 cups of stock into a large saucepan and bring to the boil. Add the roasted vegetables and return to the boil. Remove from the heat and use a stick blender to blend until smooth, or process in a food processor in batches until smooth.

3 Check the consistency, adding more stock if needed. Return to medium heat and bring to the boil. Taste, adjust seasoning and serve with toast.

Oven-roasted mushrooms

Packed full of flavour and nutrients, I just love this dish – I hope you will too.

Serves 4 as a main

12 small flat mushrooms, stems trimmed

100g ricotta

100g goat's cheese or marinated feta

2 garlic cloves, crushed

1 tablespoon rosemary leaves

200g roasted red capsicum, chopped
    (see page 46)

2½ tablespoons extra-virgin olive oil

1 tablespoon balsamic glaze
    (see page 120) ★

100g baby rocket or spinach leaves

sourdough toast, to serve

★ Balsamic glaze will keep in a clean jar at room temperature for 3 months. Warm it in the microwave for 20–30 seconds on High/100%.

1 Place a roasting pan in the oven. Preheat the oven and pan to 200°C fan-forced. Place the mushrooms stem side up on a board.

2 Beat the ricotta and goat's cheese together until well combined. Add garlic, rosemary and capsicum and stir until well combined. Dollop the mixture evenly over the mushrooms.

3 Remove the hot pan from the oven and swirl 2 teaspoons of oil over the base of the pan. Add the mushrooms and drizzle over 1 tablespoon of the remaining oil, then season with salt and pepper. Roast for 15 minutes, or until mushrooms are tender.

4 Combine the balsamic glaze and the remaining 1 tablespoon of oil in a bowl. Season with salt and pepper, add rocket and toss to coat. Remove the mushrooms from the oven, scatter over the dressed rocket and serve warm with crusty bread as a main or as side with beef, chicken or fish.

Vegetable san choy bau

A vegetarian dinner once or twice a week is good for us all. Serve this up and no one will ask where the meat is. (But if they do, add shredded chicken or cooked peeled prawns.)

Serves 2 as a main

2 carrots, peeled

2 sticks celery

1 bunch asparagus, trimmed

1 red capsicum, quartered

125g snow peas, topped

1 tablespoon hoisin sauce

2 tablespoons Shaoxing Chinese
   cooking wine

1 teaspoon brown sugar

¼ teaspoon sesame oil

1 tablespoon peanut oil

2cm piece ginger, finely grated

2 garlic cloves, crushed

1 long red chilli, seeds removed,
   finely chopped

100g fresh mushrooms (such as shiitake
   & Swiss brown), stems discarded,
   thinly sliced

1 cup bean sprouts, trimmed

6 small iceberg lettuce leaves ♥

fried eschalots, to serve

1 Using a vegetable peeler, thinly slice the carrots lengthways into ribbons. Cut the ribbons in half crossways and then, using a sharp knife, cut into long thin strips and place in a bowl. Cut the celery, asparagus, capsicum and snow peas into similar size strips to the carrot. Place the celery, asparagus and capsicum in the bowl with the carrots, leaving the snow peas to one side.

2 Combine the hoisin, wine, sugar and sesame oil in a bowl and set aside.

3 Heat the wok over high heat until hot. Add the peanut oil and swirl to coat. Add all the vegetables in the bowl, then the ginger, garlic and chilli, and stir-fry for 1 minute, until fragrant. Add the mushrooms and stir-fry for a further 1 minute. Pour the hoisin sauce mixture over the vegetables and stir-fry for 30 seconds. Add the snow peas and bean sprouts, toss to combine, and then remove from the heat.

4 Spoon the vegetables into the lettuce cups, sprinkle with fried eschalots and serve.

♥ To separate the leaves, bash the core of the lettuce hard on a board to loosen it. Then, holding the lettuce in one hand and the core firmly in the other, twist the core to remove it. Place the lettuce in a large bowl of iced water to crisp up and separate the leaves. Pat dry with paper towel or spin in a salad spinner.

Mushroom baked gnocchi
with garlic croutons

As you can imagine, we eat very well when we are shooting the pics for this book. When this came out of the oven we couldn't shoot it quickly enough – though it was still only 11 o'clock, we called it early lunch!

Serves 4

2 tablespoons olive oil

1 leek, halved lengthways, rinsed, dried, thinly sliced

400g mushrooms, sliced (I use buttons & Swiss brown)

300ml thickened cream

¼ cup fresh flat-leaf parsley, chopped

650g potato or ricotta gnocchi (see page 126)

Garlic croutons

4 slices sourdough, torn into pieces

2 tablespoons olive oil

2 garlic cloves, crushed

1 lemon, rind finely grated

1 Heat the oil in a non-stick frying pan over medium heat. Add the leek and cook for 3–4 minutes, until soft. Add the mushrooms, increase the heat to high and cook for 8 minutes, or until tender. Stir in the cream and simmer for 10 minutes, until sauce reduces and thickens slightly. Stir in the parsley.

2 Preheat the oven to 200°C fan-forced. Lightly grease a 6-cup capacity baking dish (5cm deep, 16cm × 23cm).

3 Cook the gnocchi in a large saucepan of boiling, salted water for 2 minutes, or until partially cooked. ★ Drain and spoon into the prepared dish, then pour over the mushroom sauce, season with salt and pepper and stir gently to coat the gnocchi. Place the gnocchi in the oven and bake for 18–20 minutes, until piping hot.

4 Meanwhile, for the garlic croutons, place the pieces of sourdough on a baking tray, combine the oil, garlic and lemon rind in a bowl, then spoon over the bread, turn to coat. Place the tray with the bread pieces onto an oven shelf under the gnocchi and cook for 8–10 minutes, until golden and crisp.

5 Scatter the crisp crumbs over the gnocchi and serve.

★ It's important not to overcook the gnocchi at this stage, as it goes back into oven for 20 minutes in a later step of the recipe. There's nothing worse than gluggy gnocchi!

Sticky chicken wings with corn & avocado salad

Serves 4

¼ cup port
¼ cup redcurrant jelly
2 tablespoons brown sugar
4cm piece ginger, grated
1 teaspoon Chinese five-spice powder
1 tablespoon olive oil
12–16 chicken wings

Corn & avocado salad

¼ cup extra-virgin olive oil
1 tablespoon cider vinegar
1 teaspoon caster sugar
3 corncobs, husk on
2 avocados, peeled, chopped
1 cup baby Asian salad mix

1 Combine the port, redcurrant jelly, sugar and ginger in a small saucepan over medium heat. Cook, stirring often, for 5–8 minutes, until the jelly melts and the marinade thickens slightly. Remove from the heat, stir in the five-spice and oil and set aside to cool.

2 Use a sharp knife to cut the wingtips off at the joint. ♥ Place the wings in a snap lock bag. Pour the marinade over the chicken and rub the bag carefully to coat all the wings. Seal and refrigerate for 30 minutes if time permits.

3 Preheat the oven to 200°C fan-forced. Drain the excess marinade from the chicken into a saucepan and bring to the boil over high heat. Boil gently for 5 minutes. Place the wings in a roasting pan lined with baking paper. Roast the chicken, basting every 10 minutes with the cooked marinade, for 30–40 minutes, or until the chicken is sticky and cooked through.

4 Meanwhile, for the corn and avocado salad, whisk the oil, vinegar, sugar and salt and pepper together in a bowl. Carefully peel back the corn husks and remove the fine silks. Reposition the husks back over the corn. ★ Tie with string to secure. Soak the corn in a bowl of cold water for 5 minutes. Drain well, shaking the corn. Microwave the corncobs for 5–6 minutes on High/100%, until kernels are just tender. Remove the husks and set aside to cool for 5 minutes. Cut the warm kernels from the cob and add to the dressing, stir to coat, and set aside to cool to room temperature. Add the avocado and Asian salad mix just before serving and toss gently to coat. Serve with the sticky chicken wings.

♥ Wingtips make great chicken stock. If you don't have the time right away, freeze them in a snap lock bag, but don't forget they are there.

★ If there's no husk on the corn, remove the silks, wash the corn and wrap it loosely in microwave-safe plastic wrap.

Lemon & garlic roast chicken

. . . .

Sometimes a recipe looks too simple to be flavoursome, but don't be fooled – this one is sensational.

Serves 4

¼ cup extra-virgin olive oil

1 large lemon, juiced

3 large garlic cloves, crushed

1 tablespoon honey

8 pieces chicken ♥

500g Lady Crystal or desiree potatoes

1 tablespoon olive oil

2 tablespoons flat-leaf parsley,
  roughly chopped

♥ In the photograph I have used chicken cutlets, which are the thigh meat on the bone with the skin removed. You could also use marylands, or a whole chicken cut into eight.

1 Combine the extra-virgin olive oil, lemon juice, garlic and honey in a screw-top jar. Season with salt and pepper and shake well to combine.

2 Place the chicken in a ceramic dish, pour over one-third of the marinade and turn to coat, rubbing into the chicken with your fingertips. Cover chicken and refrigerate for 15 minutes if time permits. Set the remaining marinade aside for later.

3 Pierce the potatoes with a fork 4 times, then place on the outer edge of the microwave turntable. Microwave for 5 minutes on High/100%. They should still be firm. Wrap in a tea towel and set aside for 10 minutes.

4 Preheat the oven to 200°C fan-forced. Cut the potatoes into chunks and place in a large roasting pan. Drizzle with the olive oil and roast for 10 minutes.

5 Meanwhile, heat a large non-stick frying pan over high heat. Cook the chicken, in batches, for 2 minutes on each side, until golden. Place the chicken in the roasting pan with the potatoes and pour over the reserved lemon and garlic marinade. Roast for 20–25 minutes, turning the chicken and potatoes occasionally, until the chicken is cooked through and the potatoes golden and crisp. Sprinkle over the parsley and serve with fennel and pear salad (see page 42).

Cajun chicken

If you are lucky enough to have a lemon tree of your own, or if a neighbour has one, the branches make great skewers for these chicken kebabs.

Serves 4

800g chicken thigh fillets, trimmed
2 tablespoons olive oil
1 lemon, juiced
2 lemons, cut into wedges
steamed rice or corn tortillas, to serve

Cajun spice rub ★

3 teaspoons cumin seeds
3 teaspoons coriander seeds
3 teaspoons fennel seeds
3 teaspoons sweet paprika
3 teaspoons mustard powder
3 teaspoons onion powder
3 teaspoons ground oregano
½ teaspoon garlic powder
½ teaspoon brown sugar
good pinch cayenne pepper

Minted peas

1½ cups fresh or frozen peas
2 tablespoons olive oil
¼ cup mint leaves, finely shredded
½ teaspoon caster sugar

1 For the Cajun spice rub, combine the cumin, coriander and fennel seeds in a small non-stick frying pan over medium heat. Cook, gently shaking the pan, for 4–5 minutes, or until the seeds start to pop or the mixture grows fragrant. Remove from the heat and transfer to a mortar. Cool for 5 minutes, then use a pestle to pound to fine powder. Transfer to a bowl, add the remaining ingredients and mix well.

2 Cut the chicken into pieces and thread onto twelve stripped lemon branches or skewers. Combine ¼ cup of the spice rub, oil and lemon juice in a shallow ceramic dish. Add chicken and turn to coat. Cover and refrigerate for 15 minutes if time permits. Thread a lemon leaf, if using, and a lemon wedge onto both ends of each skewer.

3 Preheat a barbecue plate on medium-high heat. Remove the skewers from the marinade and barbecue, turning occasionally, for 10–15 minutes, or until cooked through.

4 Meanwhile, for the minted peas, cook the peas in a saucepan of boiling salted water for 2–4 minutes, until bright green and tender. Drain well. Heat the oil in a non-stick frying pan over medium heat. Add the mint leaves and sugar and cook for 1–2 minutes, until warm. Add the peas and toss to coat in the warm minted oil. Season with salt and pepper. Serve the skewers with peas and rice or tortillas.

★ This spice rub will keep for up to one month in an airtight jar in a cool, dark place out of direct sunlight. Homemade is great, but if you want to buy it ready-made, the very best one available can be purchased online from www.herbies.com.au.

Open chicken, avocado & cheese fingers

Toasted 'fingers', as we used to call them, hit the spot for lunch or dinner any day of the week.

Serves 2

1 loaf uncut multigrain bread
2 tablespoons whole egg mayonnaise
2 teaspoons Dijon mustard
200g cooked chicken, shredded ♥
1 large ripe avocado, peeled, mashed
150g Swiss cheese, thinly sliced

♥ Any cooked chicken is suitable for this recipe. I am a big fan of smoked chicken, available in the meat section at most supermarkets.

1 Position a rack on the top shelf of the oven. Preheat the grill to high heat. Cut 4 thick slices from the loaf of bread. Place the bread on a tray and grill for 2–3 minutes, or until toasted, then remove to a serving board, un-toasted side up.

2 Reduce the grill heat to medium and re-position the oven rack one shelf lower in the oven.

3 Combine the mayonnaise, mustard and salt and pepper in a bowl, then mix until well combined. Add the chicken and stir to coat. Thickly spread the un-toasted side of each piece of bread with avocado right to the corners. Top with the chicken mixture, followed by the cheese. Place on the tray and grill for 4–5 minutes, or until the cheese is melted. Serve.

Red duck curry

Duck used to be considered gourmet, but it's now readily available, making it more affordable and everyday. Cooked barbecue duck is half the price from Asian grocery stores. If you are lucky enough to live near one, check it out. If not, some supermarkets and greengrocers are now selling the Luv-a-Duck brand – it's fabulous. Duck meat is rich, so you only need about 100g per person.

Serves 4

1 stalk lemongrass, chopped
4cm piece ginger, sliced
1 teaspoon peanut oil
3 tablespoons red curry paste
400ml can coconut cream or milk, unshaken
2 cups chicken stock
1 Chinese barbecue duck or 400g cooked duck breasts, skin & bones removed, coarsely chopped
¼ cup fish sauce
2 tablespoons grated palm sugar
1 large lime, juiced
565g can lychees, drained
1 bunch baby bok choy, shredded ★
½ cup Thai basil leaves, optional
cooked fresh rice noodles, to serve

★ When you shred the leaves and stems, keep them separate, as the stems need to be cooked a little longer than the leaves.

1 Place the lemongrass and ginger in a small food processor or mortar and pestle and process or pound to a paste.

2 Heat a wok over medium-high heat until hot. Add the oil and swirl to coat the wok. Add the red curry paste and lemongrass paste and cook, stirring, for 20 seconds, or until aromatic. Add the thick top layer from the can of coconut cream or milk and cook for 1 minute, or until it splits (this is known as cracking the milk). Add the remaining coconut cream or milk and chicken stock and bring to the boil. Reduce the heat to low and simmer for 5 minutes, or until reduced slightly.

3 Add the duck and simmer for 3 minutes. Combine the fish sauce, palm sugar and 3 tablespoons of lime juice and stir into the curry with the lychees and bok choy stems. Simmer for 3 minutes, then remove from the heat. Add the bok choy leaves and stir to combine. Scatter over the basil leaves, if using, and serve over noodles.

Middle Eastern chicken

This is a great Friday night dinner. Served in a big bowl with a fork, it's better than any take-out!

Serves 4

¼ cup plain flour

1 teaspoon sweet paprika

500g chicken thigh fillet or breast,
    cut into 2cm pieces

¼ cup olive oil

2 brown onions, halved, thinly sliced

2 teaspoons ground cinnamon

1 teaspoon ground cumin

1 teaspoon ground coriander

1 cup chicken stock

⅓ cup sultanas

1 lemon, halved

¼ cup slivered almonds, toasted

2 tablespoons flat-leaf parsley, chopped

couscous & Greek yoghurt, to serve

1 Combine the flour, paprika and salt and pepper in a snap lock bag. Add the chicken and toss to coat. Heat a large frying pan over medium-high heat until hot. Add 1 tablespoon of oil and half the chicken, then cook for 2–3 minutes, until browned. Remove to a plate and repeat with the oil and the remaining chicken.

2 Reduce the heat to medium-low and add the remaining oil to the pan with the onions. Cook, stirring often, for 8 minutes, until softened. Add the cinnamon, cumin and coriander and cook for 30 seconds. Return all the chicken and any juices to the pan. Add the stock and sultanas and cook for 5 minutes, or until the chicken is cooked through.

3 Squeeze over the juice of one lemon half and stir gently to combine. Remove from the heat and stir in the almonds and parsley. Serve with couscous, yoghurt and the remaining lemon.

Smoked salmon pâté

I am not a fan of chicken liver pâté – I wish I was – but I do love a cocktail party and a good easy starter. Though there are rarely any leftovers when I dish this up, if you have any, it's delicious on wraps or sandwiches instead of butter.

Serves 4

300g smoked salmon, chopped

2 green onions, thinly sliced

¾ cup crème fraîche

¼ cup whole egg mayonnaise

1 tablespoon dill, finely chopped

½ lime, juiced

3 teaspoons horseradish cream

4–8 small fresh bay leaves

80g clarified butter, melted ♥

oven-baked sourdough bread, to serve

1 Place the salmon and green onions in a food processor and process until finely chopped. Add the crème fraîche and mayonnaise and pulse until almost smooth. Transfer to a bowl.

2 Add the dill, lime juice and horseradish and gently stir until combined. Taste and season with salt and pepper. Spoon the salmon mixture evenly into 4 × ½-cup capacity ramekins and smooth the surface.

3 Place the bay leaves on top of the pâté and pour over 1 tablespoon of melted butter. Refrigerate for 4 hours, or overnight if time permits. Serve with oven-baked sourdough.

♥ Clarified butter or ghee is butter that's been heated to separate the water content from the fat. The water is then drained off, leaving a bright yellow butter that can be cooked to a higher temperature without burning.

Crispy skin barramundi with roasted cauliflower salad

Serves 4

1 tablespoon olive oil

40g butter, chopped

4 pieces barramundi, skin on,
   bones removed

1 lemon, rind shredded, juiced

Roasted cauliflower salad

500g cauliflower, washed, sliced

olive oil cooking spray

2 tablespoons extra-virgin olive oil

1 teaspoon ground turmeric

2 teaspoons ground cumin

1 teaspoon fennel seeds, bruised

½ teaspoon ground cinnamon

½ cup apple or pear juice

1 small red onion, halved,
   very thinly sliced

¼ cup flat-leaf parsley, chopped

2 tablespoons flaked almonds, toasted

1 For the roasted cauliflower salad, preheat the oven to 200°C fan-forced. Scatter the cauliflower over the base of a large roasting pan. Spray with oil and season with salt and pepper. Roast for 12–15 minutes, until light golden and just tender. Set aside to cool for 10 minutes.

2 Meanwhile, heat the extra-virgin olive oil in a small non-stick frying pan over medium heat. Add the turmeric, cumin, fennel and cinnamon and cook for 1 minute, or until aromatic. Remove from the heat, then add apple juice and swirl to combine. Transfer the warm cauliflower to a bowl, pour over the warm spiced apple mixture and toss gently to combine.

3 Heat a large non-stick frying pan over high heat until hot. Add half the oil and half the butter and swirl until the butter is melted. Season both sides of the fish with salt and pepper. Cook 2 pieces of fish, skin side down, for 3–4 minutes, or until skin is crisp. ★ Turn and cook a further 1–2 minutes, or until the fish is cooked through. Remove to a plate and cover to keep warm. Repeat with the remaining oil, butter and fish. Add the lemon rind and juice to the hot pan and swirl to coat.

4 Add the onion, parsley and almonds to the cauliflower and toss gently to combine. Spoon onto serving plates, then top with fish, spoon over the pan juices and serve.

★ Score the skin two or three times with a sharp knife to prevent it from curling, and once you have added the fish to the pan, press down on the flesh with spatula for 30 seconds. This helps colour and crisp up the skin.

Prawn & watermelon salad

The combination of prawns and watermelon is simply divine. This salad doubles as a main on a warm summer night or as a side on any barbecue or Christmas buffet table.

Serves 4

750g cooked prawns, peeled, deveined

1kg seedless watermelon, peeled, chopped

100g baby spinach leaves

½ cup walnuts, toasted, chopped

¼ cup mint leaves, finely shredded

125g Greek feta

1 tablespoon sesame seeds, toasted

crusty bread, to serve

Dressing

3 tablespoons extra-virgin olive oil

1 lime, juiced ♥

3 teaspoons honey

1 teaspoon Dijon mustard

♥ To get more juice from a citrus fruit, roll it on a benchtop before you cut it open, or microwave it for 15 seconds on High/100%.

1 For the dressing, combine the oil, 1½ tablespoons of lime juice and the honey and mustard together in a heat-proof microwave-safe bowl. Microwave, uncovered, on High/100% for 15 seconds to dissolve the honey. Season with salt and pepper and whisk until well combined. Set aside to cool.

2 Combine the prawns, watermelon, spinach, walnuts and mint in a bowl. Crumble over the feta.

3 Pour the dressing over the salad just before serving and toss gently to combine. Sprinkle over the sesame seeds and serve with crusty bread as a main.

Chilli, mint & lime seared salmon

Quick, easy, healthy and super-delicious, I have no doubt this dish will become a regular midweek meal in your home.

Serves 4

800g salmon fillet, skin removed
1 teaspoon dried chilli flakes
3 garlic cloves, crushed
⅓ cup mint leaves, chopped
⅓ cup olive oil
1 lime, juiced

Papaya & cucumber salad

1 green papaya, peeled, quartered
3 Lebanese cucumbers
½ cup fresh mint leaves
¼ cup Greek yoghurt
1 lime, juiced
2 teaspoons water
1 teaspoon brown sugar

1 Cut the salmon into pieces. Combine the chilli, garlic, mint, olive oil and lime juice in a ceramic dish. Season with salt and pepper. Add the salmon and turn to coat. Cover and refrigerate for no longer than 10 minutes. ♥

2 For the papaya and cucumber salad, peel the papaya into long thin ribbons with a potato peeler, then finely shred and place in a bowl. Peel the cucumber into long thin ribbons with a potato peeler, then add to the papaya with the mint. Combine the yoghurt, 2 tablespoons of lime juice, the water and brown sugar in a screw-top jar. Shake until well combined. Pour the dressing over the salad and toss gently to combine.

3 Preheat a barbecue grill on high heat. Thread the salmon onto 4 long metal skewers or 8 bamboo skewers. Barbecue the salmon, basting and turning occasionally, for 4 minutes for medium, or until cooked to your liking.

4 Serve the salmon with papaya and cucumber salad.

♥ The acid in the lime juice will quickly start to 'cook' the salmon. Don't leave it to marinate too long, or the texture of the flesh will deteriorate.

Prawn & antipasto spaghetti

It's common to think of prawns as a specialty food, but they are often cheaper per kilo than many cuts of meat and chicken – granted, you lose almost half the weight once they're peeled, but they're so good for you and a little goes a long way in this recipe. Give this a try midweek.

Serves 4

400g spaghetti

⅓ cup extra-virgin olive oil

1 large lemon, rind finely grated

750g cooked prawns, peeled, deveined

5 green onions, thinly sliced

500g antipasto (such as semi-dried
   tomatoes, char-grilled eggplant,
   roasted capsicum, stuffed olives,
   balsamic mushrooms), chopped

¼ cup basil leaves, shredded

125g wedge ricotta

1 Cook the spaghetti in a large saucepan of boiling salted water, following packet directions, until al dente.

2 Meanwhile, whisk the oil and lemon rind together. Set aside while the pasta is cooking.

3 Drain the pasta and transfer to a large bowl. Pour over the lemon oil and toss gently to coat while the pasta is warm. Add the prawns, green onions, antipasto and basil. Cut the lemon in half and squeeze over the pasta, then toss gently to combine. Season with salt and pepper and arrange on a serving plate. Crumble over the ricotta and serve.

Barbecue lamb with lemon curd dressing

Ready Steady Cook *is a great learning place for us all. In 2009, Jared Ingersoll from Danks Street Depot and I teamed up on set. Jared added my curd to his dressing and thus this winning dish was created.*

Serves 4

½ lemon, juiced

3 garlic cloves, crushed

1 tablespoon rosemary leaves, chopped

1 tablespoon thyme leaves

1 tablespoon flat-leaf parsley, chopped

8 large lamb loin chops, trimmed

Lemon curd dressing

2 tablespoons lemon curd (see page 79)

1 tablespoon extra-virgin olive oil

1 tablespoon lemon juice

1–2 tablespoons warm water

1 Combine the lemon juice, garlic, herbs and salt and pepper in a ceramic dish. Add the lamb and turn to coat both sides. Cover and refrigerate for 10 minutes if time permits.

2 For the lemon curd dressing, combine the lemon curd, oil, lemon juice and salt and pepper in a screw-top jar and shake to combine. Add enough warm water to the dressing to give it the consistency of pouring cream. ♥

3 Preheat a barbecue plate or large non-stick frying pan over medium-high heat. Remove the lamb from the marinade and cook, basting occasionally, for 4–5 minutes on each side for medium, or until cooked to your liking. Transfer to a tray, cover with foil and set aside to rest for 5 minutes.

4 Spoon the dressing over the lamb and serve with minted peas (see page 19).

♥ The amount of water you need will depend on how thick the lemon curd is. You can use bought lemon curd – it usually has a runnier consistency than homemade.

Quick lamb, haloumi & pinenut pizza

I usually make pizza dough from scratch, but I was served this pizza recently in a little Greek cafe and it's pretty fabulous. The secret is to squash the bread – this produces a thin, crusty base that's easy to eat.

Makes 4

1 Lebanese cucumber, halved lengthways
¾ cup Greek yoghurt
2 tablespoons mint leaves, shredded
2 tablespoons olive oil
1 brown onion, finely chopped
2 garlic cloves, crushed
2–3 teaspoons ground sumac
375g lamb mince
2 Turkish bread rolls, split
olive oil cooking spray
¼ cup pine nuts
100g haloumi, grated
tabbouleh salad, to serve

Hummos
¼ cup extra-virgin olive oil
400g can chickpeas, rinsed, drained
1 tablespoon organic tahini
2 garlic cloves, crushed
½ lemon, juiced

1 For the hummos, combine all the ingredients in a food processor and process until smooth. Season with salt and pepper. Spoon into a bowl, press a piece of plastic wrap right onto the surface, then cover the bowl and refrigerate until required.

2 Use a teaspoon to scrape the seeds from the cucumber halves. Discard the seeds, dice the flesh and place in a bowl. Add the yoghurt and mint, then season with salt and pepper. Cover and refrigerate until ready to serve.

3 Heat oil in a non-stick frying pan over medium heat, add the onion and garlic and cook for 5 minutes, until soft. Add sumac and cook for 1 minute. Increase the heat to high and add the mince. Cook, stirring occasionally with a wooden spoon, for 8–10 minutes, or until the mince changes colour. Set aside to cool for 10 minutes.

4 Preheat the oven and a large flat baking tray to 230°C fan-forced. Place the bread roll halves in a cold sandwich press and press to flatten, so they are paper thin. ★ Spray both sides of the bread rolls with olive oil spray.

5 Spread the cut side of the rolls with hummos. Drain the moisture from the mince, then spoon over the hummos. Scatter the pine nuts and grated haloumi on top, then place on the hot tray and bake for 5–8 minutes, or until the bases are crisp. Spoon over the tabbouleh, top with a dollop of yoghurt mixture and serve.

★ If you don't have a sandwich press, you can roll the bread with a rolling pin to flatten it.

Char-grilled pork with fennel & pear salad

Pork with fennel and pear is a great combination. I love to add fresh figs or thinly sliced dried figs to the salad when I have them.

Serves 4

1 tablespoon fennel seeds

2 teaspoons sea salt flakes

1 tablespoon extra-virgin olive oil

2 tablespoon fig paste or fig jam

4 pork loin cutlets

Fennel & pear salad

1 medium bulb fennel, trimmed,
   halved lengthways

2 firm pears, halved, cored

2 tablespoons pear juice

¼ cup extra-virgin olive oil

60g baby spinach or rocket leaves

1 Place the fennel seeds in a small non-stick frying pan over medium-high heat for 3 minutes, shaking the pan often, until aromatic. Transfer to a mortar, add the sea salt flakes and pound with a pestle until roughly crushed, or use the end of a rolling pin to crush the seeds and salt together.

2 Combine the extra-virgin olive oil and fig paste or jam together, then rub over both sides of the pork. Sprinkle over fennel and salt mixture.

3 Preheat a barbecue plate or char-grill on medium-high. Cook the pork for 4 minutes on each side, or until just cooked through. Transfer to a plate, cover with foil and set aside for 5 minutes to rest.

4 For the fennel and pear salad, thinly slice the fennel and pears (using a mandolin is the best way to do this) and place in a bowl. Combine the pear juice, extra-virgin olive oil and salt and pepper in a screw-top jar and shake well. Pour the dressing over the fennel and pears and toss to combine. Cover and refrigerate for 10 minutes if time permits. Add spinach or rocket just before serving and toss again.

5 Serve the pork chops with the fennel and pear salad.

Pork larb

This is one of those delicious versatile dishes – serve it warm as a substantial main, or replace the noodles with a baguette or bread roll spread with sweet chilli sauce and pile on some cold pork for lunch.

Serves 4

2 garlic cloves, crushed

1cm piece ginger, chopped

1 long fresh red chilli, seeds removed, chopped

1 stick lemongrass, white part only, chopped

1 tablespoon salted roasted peanuts

2 tablespoons fish sauce

3 teaspoons grated palm sugar

1 lime, juiced

1 tablespoon peanut oil

500g pork mince

100g vermicelli noodles

100g bean sprouts, trimmed ★

1 cup coriander leaves

1 cup mint leaves

butter lettuce leaves, to serve

★ Unused bean sprouts should be kept in a bowl of cold water in the fridge. They will stay crisp for up to 5 days.

1 Combine the garlic, ginger, chilli, lemongrass and peanuts in a small food processor and process until very finely chopped, or pound in a mortar with a pestle. Combine the fish sauce, palm sugar and 2 tablespoons of lime juice in a jug, stir to dissolve the sugar, then set aside.

2 Heat a wok over high heat until very hot. Add the oil and swirl to coat the wok's surface. Add the pork mince and stir-fry for 6–8 minutes, or until the pork changes colour. Add the garlic mixture and stir-fry for 1 minute. Add the lime juice mixture and stir to coat. Remove from the heat and set aside for 5 minutes to allow the pork to absorb the lime mixture.

3 Meanwhile, place the noodles in a heat-proof bowl, cover with boiling water and stand for 1–2 minutes to soften. Drain well.

4 Add the bean sprouts, coriander and mint to the pork and toss gently to combine. Place a lettuce leaf in each bowl, then top with noodles and the pork mixture and serve.

Chorizo with lentils & roasted red capsicum

I was lucky enough to travel around Spain with the Spanish Olive Oil Council. I've never eaten so much and slept so little on a trip. Planted firmly on a bar stool, this is one of the many dishes the locals insisted we try.

Serves 4

2 tablespoons olive oil

2 large garlic cloves, thinly sliced

4 chorizo sausages, roughly chopped

400g can brown lentils, drained, rinsed

1 teaspoon smoked paprika

400g can diced tomatoes

2 bay leaves

1 cup chicken stock

toasted crusty bread, to serve

Roasted red capsicum

2 large red capsicums

1 For the roasted red capsicum, cut the capsicums in quarters and remove the core and seeds. Preheat a grill on high. Place the capsicum skin side up on a baking tray and grill for 6–8 minutes, or until the skin turns black. Transfer the capsicum to a snap lock bag and seal, then let stand for 5 minutes. (The steam helps to lift the skin.) Use your fingers to peel and remove the skin. (Don't rinse the capsicum under cold water as this dilutes the flavour.) Place in a bowl and set aside.

2 Heat a heavy-based frying pan over medium heat until hot. Add the oil and garlic slices and cook for 4 minutes or until garlic is golden. Tip the garlic oil into a small heat-proof bowl. Add the chorizo to the hot pan and cook for 6–8 minutes, turning, until light golden.

3 Add the lentils. Sprinkle over the paprika and stir to coat. Add the tomatoes, bay leaves and stock, then reduce heat to low and cook for 15 minutes until thickened.

4 Remove the bay leaves. Cut the roasted capsicum into strips and stir into the pan. Spoon into ramekins or bowls, spoon over the warm garlic and oil and serve with toasted crusty bread.

Curry in a hurry

This is not the most attractive dish to look at – I even considered dropping it from the book for that reason – but it just tastes too good, and it only uses one pan.

Serves 4

1 cucumber, peeled, halved lengthways
2 carrots, peeled
2 green onions, trimmed
8 pork sausages (Peppercorn brand)
olive oil cooking spray
3 teaspoons peanut oil
1 small red onion, cut into thin wedges
2-3 tablespoons curry paste ♥
1 cup coconut milk
steamed rice & pappadums, to serve

♥ You can use any curry paste you like – balti, massaman or even red or green curry paste.

1 Use a teaspoon to remove the seeds from the cucumber. Cut the cucumber, carrots and green onions into long thin strips. Set aside.

2 Heat a medium non-stick frying pan over medium-high heat until hot. Cut the sausages in half lengthways, but not all the way through. Spray both sides lightly with oil and add to the hot pan, cut side down. Cook for 3 minutes, pressing down on the sausages with a spatula to keep them flat, then turn and cook for a further 2–3 minutes, until golden and just cooked through. Transfer to a plate and cover to keep warm.

3 Reduce the heat to medium and add a little oil to the hot pan if needed.★ Add the onion and cook for 1 minute, until soft. Add the curry paste and cook, stirring, for 30 seconds, until aromatic. Add the coconut milk and bring to the boil. Add the sausages and turn to coat in the sauce, then simmer for 1–2 minutes, until warmed through.

4 Place the sausages on plates, spoon over the sauce, top with vegetables and serve with rice and pappadums.

★ Depending on the sausages you use, there may be enough fat in the pan, so only add extra if you need it.

My bacon & egg roll

I can eat a bacon and egg roll any time of the day. There is a little beach cafe on Sydney's northern beaches I run to on a Sunday where it's not uncommon for me to eat a bacon and egg roll then try to run home. The secret is good sauce, crispy bacon, a fresh roll and a perfectly fried egg.

Makes 2

2 fresh bread rolls ♥

4 rashers bacon, rind removed

1 tablespoon extra-virgin olive oil

2 free-range eggs

1 lemon

lettuce leaves & marinated feta, optional,
   to serve

My bacon & egg roll sauce

¼ cup tomato sauce

¼ cup barbecue sauce

1 tablespoon Dijon mustard

1 tablespoon chilli sauce

1 tablespoon treacle

1 tablespoon water

♥ The bread rolls for this recipe need to be fresh, warm and soft. This makes them really easy to eat.

1 For my bacon and egg roll sauce, combine all the ingredients in a saucepan over medium heat. Cook, stirring, for 3–5 minutes, until the sauce comes to the boil. Set aside to cool. Taste, adjusting the chilli and sugar to suit yourself. Unused sauce will keep for 2 months in an airtight jar in the fridge.

2 Preheat the oven to 180°C fan-forced. Place the rolls in the oven and heat for 5 minutes, until warm (not crusty).

3 Meanwhile, cut the bacon rashers into thirds. Heat a non-stick frying pan over medium-high heat, add the bacon and cook for 2–3 minutes on each side, until golden. Transfer to a plate and keep warm.

4 Add oil to the pan and reduce the heat to medium. Add the eggs, cook for 1 minute for medium, or until eggs are cooked to your liking. Remove from the heat and finely grate over a little lemon rind.

5 Cut the rolls in half and spread the base with the bacon and egg roll sauce. Top with the lettuce, bacon and egg. Season with salt and freshly ground black pepper and crumble over the feta, if using. Sandwich together with the top of the bread roll and serve.

Soy & ginger beef

Shop-bought soy marinades contain preservatives and additives – but it's incredibly easy to make your own. Keep any unused marinade in a jar in the fridge for up to a month.

Serves 4

500g beef fillet steak, trimmed
2 teaspoons sesame oil
2cm piece ginger, grated
1½ tablespoons peanut oil ♥
2 carrots, peeled, cut into thin strips
2 sticks celery, cut into thin strips
1 small red capsicum, cut into thin strips
100g snow peas, thinly sliced
　　on diagonal
steamed jasmine rice or rice noodles,
　　to serve

Soy dressing

¼ cup soy sauce
2 tablespoons honey
1 garlic clove, crushed
2cm piece ginger, thinly sliced
1 small red chilli, halved, seeds removed

♥ Peanut oil is best for cooking over high heat, as it won't burn as quickly as other oils.

1 For the soy dressing, combine all the ingredients in a small saucepan over medium-high heat and bring to the boil. Boil gently for 5 minutes, stirring occasionally, until the dressing reduces by half. (It will become thick and syrupy on cooling.) Set aside to cool. Strain, discarding the ginger and chilli.

2 Thinly slice the beef across the grain (this helps keep the meat tender). Combine the sesame oil and ginger in a bowl, add the beef and stir to coat.

3 Heat the wok over high heat until hot. (Don't add the oil yet, or it will burn before the wok is hot enough for cooking.) Add 1 teaspoon of peanut oil and swirl to coat the wok. Add a quarter of the beef and stir-fry for 30 seconds, until sealed. Remove to a clean bowl. Repeat with the oil and beef in three batches. (Cooking the meat in batches means that the wok stays very hot, searing the meat, not stewing it.)

4 Add the remaining 2 teaspoons of peanut oil to the wok, then add all the vegetables and stir-fry for 1 minute. Return all the beef and any juices to the wok. Add 1–2 tablespoons of the soy dressing and stir-fry until well combined. Serve over rice or noodles.

Spiced beef tacos

These may look a little fancy, but they're really just an old family favourite, dressed up. Tacos will have a whole new lease of life on your family table once you have served these.

Serves 4

800g beef rump steak, trimmed
2 tablespoons olive oil
2 garlic cloves, crushed
1 tablespoon ground cumin
1 tablespoon ground coriander
2 teaspoons smoked paprika
¼ teaspoon cayenne pepper
1 ripe avocado, halved, mashed
soft flour tortillas, warmed ★
½ cup sour cream

Shredded salad

1 large carrot, peeled
2 small green zucchini, trimmed
4 large radishes, thinly sliced
½ cup flat-leaf parsley leaves
½ cup small mint leaves
2 tablespoons olive oil
1 lime, juiced
2 teaspoons white sugar
½ long green chilli, finely chopped
½ long red chilli, finely chopped

1 Cut the beef into cubes. Combine the oil, garlic, cumin, coriander, paprika and cayenne in a ceramic dish and mix well. Add the beef and stir to coat well. Cover and refrigerate for 5 minutes, or longer if time permits.

2 Preheat a barbecue plate or large non-stick frying pan over medium-high heat. Thread the beef onto 8 skewers. Cook, turning occasionally and basting with the marinade for 4–5 minutes for medium, or until the beef is cooked to your liking. Transfer to a plate, cover and allow to rest for 5 minutes.

3 Meanwhile, for the shredded salad, use a potato peeler to peel long thin strips from the carrot and zucchini and place in a bowl. Add radish, parsley and mint. Combine the oil, lime juice, sugar, chilli and salt and pepper in a screw-top jar and shake well to combine. Pour the dressing over the salad and toss gently to combine.

4 Spread the mashed avocado over the base of the warm tortillas. Top with a dollop of sour cream, beef and pile of shredded salad. If you're serving kids, remove the beef from the skewers before serving.

★ You can use soft shell flour tortillas or corn taco shells in this recipe – it's delicious with both. Soft tortillas can be warmed in the microwave by placing a sheet of damp paper towel between each one and then microwaving for 30 seconds on Medium/50% per tortilla. Corn shells are best warmed in the conventional oven.

Roadhouse steak with onion rings

There is something pretty special about taking a road trip with the family. We would no sooner be out the driveway than one of us would say, 'How long to go?' Mum and Dad would just roll their eyes and say, 'Not long now.' Two best memories are playing I-spy (and cheating, of course) and stopping at the roadside diner in Murwillumbah for the huge bowl of onion rings that came with the steak.

Serves 4

3 large garlic cloves, crushed
2 French shallots, finely chopped
3 tablespoons Worcestershire sauce
1 tablespoon olive oil
4 rib-eye steaks, on the bone ♥
hot English mustard & green salad,
   to serve

Onion rings
3 brown onions, peeled, thinly sliced
   into rings
½ cup buttermilk
peanut or vegetable oil, for deep-frying
½ cup plain flour

♥ Rib-eye on the bone can really vary in weight. If possible, you're looking for 4 × 350g steaks.

1 Combine the garlic, shallots, Worcestershire sauce, oil and lots of freshly ground black pepper in a shallow ceramic dish. Add the steaks and turn to coat. Cover and refrigerate for 10 minutes, or longer if time permits.

2 For the onion rings, carefully separate the sliced onions into rings and place in a ceramic bowl, pour over the buttermilk, cover and refrigerate for 15 minutes. ★

3 Preheat a barbecue plate or char-grill pan on medium-high heat. Remove the steaks from the marinade. Cook the steaks for 4 minutes, then turn and cook for 1 minute. Reduce the heat to medium and cook for a further 5–7 minutes for medium-rare, or until cooked to your liking. Place on a plate, loosely cover with foil and set aside to rest for 15 minutes.

4 Half fill a heavy-based saucepan or wok with oil and heat over medium-high heat until hot. Drain the onions from the milk. Tip the flour into a snap lock bag and season well with salt and pepper. Add the onion rings and toss to coat – don't shake off the excess. Drop the onion rings into hot oil in small batches and deep-fry for 4–5 minutes, until golden. Remove to a wire rack to drain.

5 Smear mustard over the steak, and thickly slice. Serve with the onion rings and salad.

★ The buttermilk draws out the bitterness from the onions as well as tenderising them. You can use regular milk but you will need to soak the onions for about 2 hours.

Parsley & lemon crusted sirloin

Serves 4

2 lemons, rind finely grated

2 garlic cloves, crushed

1cm piece ginger, grated

½ cup flat-leaf parsley, chopped

2 tablespoons extra-virgin olive oil

3 sirloin steaks (about 220g each), trimmed

300g green beans, trimmed

1 cup fresh or frozen peas

beetroot chutney, to serve (see page 60)

1 Combine the lemon rind, garlic, ginger, parsley and extra-virgin olive oil in a shallow ceramic dish. Add the steaks and turn to coat. Cover and refrigerate for 15 minutes if time permits.

2 Preheat the oven to 160°C fan-forced. Heat a large non-stick frying pan over medium-high heat. Add 2 steaks, cook for 2 minutes on each side to sear, then remove to a plate. Repeat with the remaining steak, then return all the steaks to the hot pan. Place the pan in the oven ★ and cook for 4 minutes for medium, or until cooked to your liking. Remove the steaks to a clean plate, reserving the pan juices. Cover the steaks to keep warm and let stand for 8 minutes.

3 Drop the beans into a saucepan of boiling salted water and cook for 1 minute. Add the peas and cook together for a further 1 minute. Drain, then arrange on a plate or platter.

4 Add 1 tablespoon of water to the pan juices and warm over medium heat. Thickly slice the steak and arrange over the beans and peas. Season with salt and pepper. Drizzle with the pan juices and serve with beetroot chutney.

★ One of the best investments you can make in the kitchen is two or three different-sized ovenproof frying pans. Searing the food in the pan traps all the juices inside, keeping it moist, and finishing it in the oven allows it to cook more gently, while still achieving a beautiful crust on both sides.

Beetroot chutney

This chutney is great to have in the fridge. It goes with almost everything, from barbecue sausages to a steak sandwich or roast chicken. It gets better the longer it's left to stand in the fridge.

Makes about 3 cups

3 medium (about 600g) beetroot, trimmed, peeled

1 apple (granny smith or golden delicious), peeled, cored

2 teaspoons olive oil

½ small red onion, thinly sliced

½ cup cider vinegar

¼ cup brown sugar

2 tablespoons treacle or golden syrup

1 teaspoon dried chilli flakes

pinch allspice powder

½ teaspoon ground cinnamon

½ teaspoon sea salt flakes

1 cup water

1 Roughly chop the beetroot and apple. Place in a food processor in batches and process until finely chopped, then transfer to a large bowl.

2 Heat the oil in a medium saucepan over medium heat, add the onion and cook for 3 minutes, until soft. Add the beetroot and apple mixture, followed by the remaining ingredients. Stir for 3–4 minutes, until the sugar and treacle dissolve. Increase the heat to medium-high and bring to the boil.

3 Boil gently for 20–25 minutes, or until the beetroot is tender and the liquid is thick and syrupy. The chutney will thicken even more on cooling.

4 Spoon the hot chutney into hot sterilised jars, seal and label. Store in the fridge for up to 6 months.

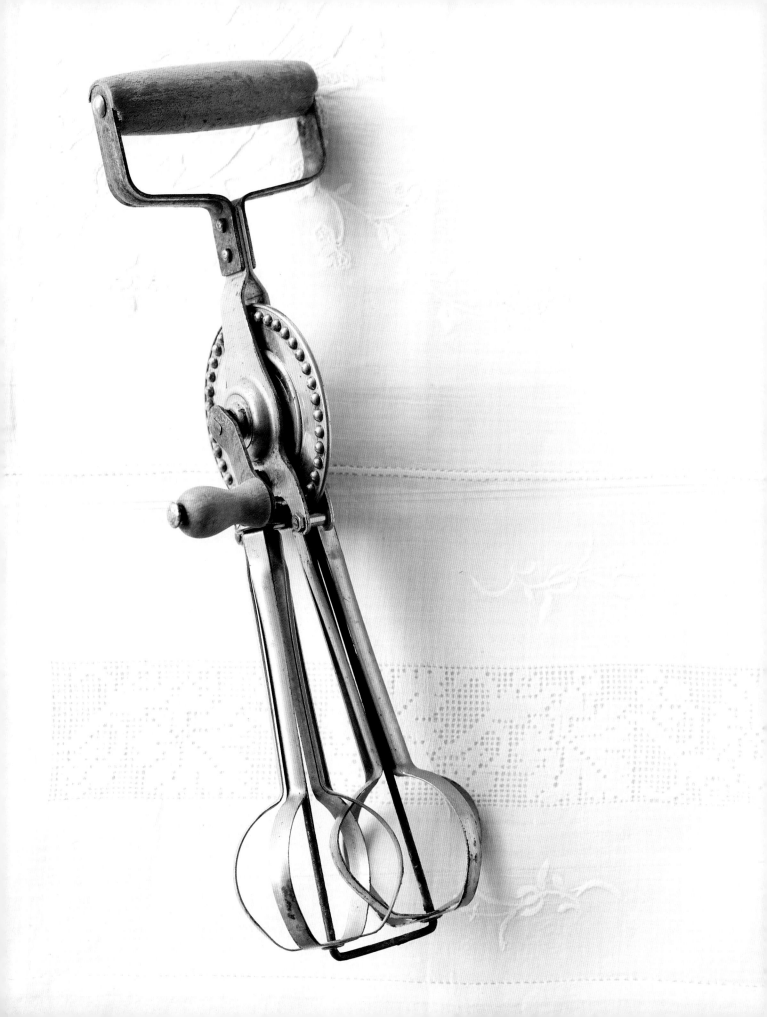

Midweek sweets

Ice-cream with chocolate sauce or canned fruit and custard is more often than not what's on offer midweek. While there's nothing wrong with that, especially if the chocolate sauce and custard are homemade, sometimes a little more effort is called for. Whether it's a family birthday, a note from school about an upcoming fundraiser, friends dropping in for a casual get-together, or just time to spoil the ones you love for no reason at all, something sweet that requires little effort with maximum results is what you want.

Custard apple & berry smoothie

Custard apples are one of the most delicious fruits available through autumn and winter. A grower once told me that because they are ugly, people don't use them, but I prefer to believe it's because we don't know what to do with them! Try this – you will love it. For a special treat, serve it with my melting moments biscuits, sandwiched together with caramel peanut butter (see page 172).

Serves 2

2 ripe custard apples, halved

1 cup frozen raspberries

1½ cups milk

½ cup Greek yoghurt

2 tablespoons honey

½ cup crushed ice

1 Scoop out the soft flesh of the custard apples with a large spoon and discard the large black seeds.

2 Spoon the fruit into a blender, then add the remaining ingredients. Blend until smooth, pour into chilled serving glasses and serve immediately.

Custard apple and mango – replace the raspberries with the chopped flesh of 2 ripe mangoes.

Custard apple, lychee & coconut – replace the raspberries with drained canned lychees and replace the milk with chilled coconut milk. Once blended, pour into a container and freeze for 1 hour, then scoop into chilled glasses.

Blender lemonade

At various times throughout the year I seem to end up with a crisper half-full of citrus that's not at its peak, so this is what I do with it. You can make this recipe with lemons, limes or oranges, or a mixture of all three. If you don't like ginger, just leave it out.

Makes 2 cups of syrup

3 lemons, washed

8cm piece ginger, unpeeled,
  ends trimmed

1½ cups white sugar

1½ cups water

ice cubes & sparkling or still
  mineral water, to serve

1 Trim the ends off each lemon. Discard the ends, then cut the lemons into 3–4 thick rounds and place in a saucepan. Cut the ginger into 8–10 pieces and place in the saucepan with the lemons.

2 Add the sugar, then pour over the water. Place over medium-high heat and bring to the boil, stirring occasionally to dissolve the sugar. Reduce the heat to medium-low and boil gently for 10 minutes. Remove from the heat and set aside to cool for 1 hour.

3 Pour the mixture into a blender and blend until well combined. Pour the mixture into a fine mesh strainer and stir to extract as much juice as possible. Pour the thick cloudy syrup into a sterilised bottle and refrigerate for up to 3 months.

4 To serve, pour syrup into the base of a glass or jug, then top with ice and sparkling or still mineral water.

For an adult version – pour 1 tablespoon of the chilled syrup into the base of a glass, add 1 tablespoon of gin, vodka or white rum and top up with ice and tonic.

Raspberry & white chocolate muffins with milkbar vanilla malt shake

Muffins can often be disappointing. I personally think they should be hot from the oven, but you know how fussy I am about perfection. Everyone I know says these are just divine cold, too.

Makes 12 muffins & 2 shakes

1²⁄₃ cups self-raising flour, sifted

²⁄₃ cup caster sugar

125g good-quality white chocolate, chopped

½ cup roasted macadamia nuts, roughly chopped

1 egg, lightly whisked

150ml buttermilk

125g butter, melted

1 cup frozen raspberries

Milkbar vanilla malt shake

2 cups icy cold milk

4 large scoops vanilla ice-cream

2 teaspoons vanilla essence

⅓ cup malt powder

1 Preheat the oven to 200°C fan-forced. Lightly grease a 12-hole, ⅓-cup capacity muffin pan, or line each hole with a large paper case. ♥

2 Combine the flour, sugar, white chocolate and macadamia nuts in a bowl and then make a well in the centre.

3 Combine the egg, buttermilk and butter in a jug, then pour into the flour mixture. Stir gently until almost combined and fold through the raspberries. Spoon evenly into the muffin cases until two-thirds full. Bake for 20–25 minutes, or until a skewer inserted into the centre comes out clean. Stand in the pan for 5 minutes, then carefully lift out.

4 Meanwhile, for the milkbar vanilla malt shake, combine all the ingredients in a blender or milkshake maker and blend until well combined. Pour into chilled glasses.

5 Serve the warm muffins with the milkbar vanilla malt shake.

♥ Paper cases prevent the muffins from sticking to the pan. If you don't use them, be sure to loosen the sides carefully with a knife and turn the muffins out after they've been standing for 3 minutes – otherwise they're likely to stick to the pan.

Cheat's almond croissants

Brunch with the family is simply awesome. We love sitting around a big table of food, talking and grazing for hours. Almond croissants are a must (mainly for me).

Makes 8

125g butter, softened
¾ cup caster sugar
1 teaspoon vanilla extract
1 egg
1½ cups ground almonds
2 tablespoons plain flour
8 croissants ★
½ cup flaked almonds
icing sugar, to serve

★ Day-old croissants are best for this recipe. You will find they are often cheaper to buy from cake shops or the bakery section of the supermarket at the end of the day. This recipe makes 12 mini or 8 regular-sized croissants.

1 Using an electric mixer, beat the butter, sugar and vanilla until pale and creamy. Add the egg and mix until well combined. Stir in the ground almonds and flour.

2 Preheat the oven to 180°C fan-forced. Slice the croissants in half horizontally, completely separating the halves. Place the croissant bases on a baking tray. Spread heaped tablespoons of almond filling over each base, then replace the croissant tops. Thickly spread 1 tablespoon of the remaining almond filling over the top of each croissant. Top with the flaked almonds, pressing down with your fingertips to secure.

3 Bake for 12–15 minutes, or until set. Serve hot, dusted with icing sugar.

Happy face biscuits with hot chocolate mallow sticks

One of the kids at Ronald McDonald House named these biscuits. 'Why happy face?' I asked. She said, 'When we make them, everyone in the house has a happy face!' The sultanas were added to try and make them a little less guilty to eat – who am I kidding!

Makes 38 biscuits & 2 hot chocolates

125g butter, softened
1¼ cups brown sugar
1 egg
¼ cup cocoa powder
¼ cup self-raising flour
1 cup plain flour
1 teaspoon bicarbonate of soda
½ cup sultanas
200g good-quality dark, milk
  or white chocolate, chopped
large packet of Smarties

Hot chocolate mallow sticks

6 marshmallows
50g milk chocolate, melted
1⅓ cups milk

1 Preheat the oven to 170°C fan-forced. Line 4 baking trays with baking paper.

2 Using an electric mixer, beat the butter and sugar until just combined. Add the egg and cocoa powder and beat until well combined. Sift the flours and bicarbonate of soda together over the chocolate mixture and mix until the dough comes together. Stir in the sultanas and chocolate.

3 Roll spoonfuls of the mixture into balls, then place on the trays, allowing room for spreading. Flatten slightly with a wet fingertip. Top with Smarties. (The biscuits spread, so be sure to add enough Smarties). ♥

4 Bake 2 trays at a time for 10 minutes, until cracked on top. Remove from the oven. If the biscuits have spread into funny shapes, use a knife to carefully push back into shape while they are hot. Stand on trays for 15 minutes, until firm enough to transfer to a wire rack to cool.

5 For the hot chocolate mallow sticks, dip half of each marshmallow into the melted chocolate and allow to set on a piece of baking paper. Push 3 marshmallows onto a skewer. Heat the milk in a saucepan or microwave until hot and pour into 2 heat-proof glasses. Insert one marshmallow skewer into each glass and serve.

♥ At Ronald McDonald house it's not uncommon for us to open the oven door after 7 minutes and quickly add few more Smarties to the top of each biscuit if we think they need them.

Sydney Electricity custard slice

My mum and aunty Faye went to cooking classes at Sydney Electricity over 45 years ago. Some of the recipes they learnt are timeless classics – like this one. Nowadays Lattice biscuits are smaller in size and there are less in the packet, so you need 2 packets for the recipe, but otherwise it's unchanged 45 years on!

Makes 16

2 × 200g packet Lattice biscuits
   (Arnott's brand)
²/₃ cup custard powder (Bingo brand)
²/₃ cup caster sugar
400ml milk
300ml thickened cream
1 teaspoon vanilla essence

Passionfruit icing

2 cups pure icing sugar
2 teaspoons butter, softened
2 passionfruit, halved

1 Line the base and sides of a 3½cm deep, 20cm × 30cm (base) slab pan with baking paper, allowing overhang along both long edges. Arrange the biscuits, lattice side down, in a single layer in the pan to cover the base, cutting the biscuits with a serrated knife to fit snugly.

2 Combine the custard powder, sugar and ½ cup milk in a saucepan. Whisk until smooth. Pour in the remaining milk and then stir in the cream and vanilla. Place the pan over medium heat and cook, stirring constantly, for 5 minutes, or until the custard comes to the boil.

3 Working quickly, pour the warm custard over the biscuits ♥ and top with another layer of biscuits, lattice side up, making sure you line them up with the biscuits on the base. Refrigerate for 1 hour, or until set.

4 For the passionfruit icing, sift the icing sugar into a microwave-safe heat-proof bowl. Add the butter and enough passionfruit pulp to make a very thick icing. Microwave, uncovered, for 40–50 seconds on High/100%, until the icing is warm and runny. Quickly pour the icing over the biscuits. Refrigerate for 1 hour, or until the icing sets. Cut the slice into squares, using the shape of the biscuits as a guide.

♥ Work quickly, so the custard doesn't set before you sandwich the second biscuit layer on top. Otherwise, the biscuits won't stick to the custard, causing the slice to fall apart when cut into pieces.

Rum, raisin & honeycomb no-bake slice

Decadent, delicious and rich – but a quick, easy way to end a meal with something special.

Makes 36

2 tablespoons dark rum

1 cup raisins

125g butter, chopped

½ cup thickened cream

500g good-quality dark chocolate,
  chopped

100g (about 8) sponge finger biscuits,
  roughly chopped

175g (1 cup) brazil nuts,
  roughly chopped

2 × 55g Crunchie chocolate bars,
  chopped

cocoa powder or icing sugar, to serve

1 Line the base and sides of a 20cm (base) square cake pan with baking paper. Place the rum in a small saucepan over medium-high heat. Heat for 2 minutes, until hot. Remove from the heat, add the raisins and stir to coat. Set aside for 20 minutes.

2 Combine the butter, cream and chocolate in a saucepan. Stir constantly over low heat with a metal spoon until just melted, or microwave in a heat-proof bowl, uncovered, in 1 minute bursts, on High/100%, stirring every minute with a metal spoon until smooth.

3 Pour three-quarters of the chocolate mixture into another large bowl. Add the raisins to the bowl with any rum that hasn't been absorbed. Then add the biscuits, brazil nuts and Crunchie bars, and stir to combine. Spoon into the cake pan and smooth the surface. Pour the remaining chocolate mixture over the top and tap the cake pan on the bench to settle the top. Cover and refrigerate until firm.

4 Lift the slice from the cake pan onto a board. Cut into pieces and dust with cocoa powder or icing sugar to serve.

Lemon meringue tartlets

These are lovely to pass around or serve plated. All three elements can be made ahead and quickly assembled just before serving.

Makes 21
1 packet Butternut Snap biscuits
   (Arnott's brand)
2 egg whites
pinch cream of tartar
½ cup caster sugar

Lemon curd
3 eggs
2 egg yolks
¾ cup caster sugar
4–5 large lemons, juiced ★
125g butter, chilled, cubed

★ You can replace the lemon juice with ¾ cup passionfruit pulp to make passionfruit curd.

1 For the lemon curd, whisk the eggs, egg yolks and sugar in a large, heat-proof, microwave-safe bowl with a balloon whisk until just combined. (Don't create too many air bubbles.) Add ¾ cup lemon juice and butter, then stir with a wooden spoon to combine. Microwave, uncovered, for 7–10 minutes on Medium/50%, whisking every minute until mixture thickens. It should thickly coat a wooden spoon dipped in. Pour the hot lemon curd into hot sterilised jars, seal and label. Refrigerate until ready to use.

2 Preheat the oven to 180°C fan-forced. Lightly grease a 12-hole round base tartlet pan. Place 12 biscuits on a baking tray. Warm in the oven for 5–8 minutes, until biscuits are soft and pliable, then quickly press them into the tartlet pan to form cups. Set aside to cool for 10 minutes, then remove to a plate. Repeat with the remaining biscuits.

3 Reduce the oven to 130°C fan-forced. Line 1 large baking tray with baking paper.

4 Using an electric mixer, beat the egg whites and cream of tartar on high speed until soft peaks form. Reduce the speed to low. Add sugar, 1 tablespoon at a time, beating constantly until well combined. After adding the final spoonful of sugar, increase the speed to high and beat for 2 minutes, or until the meringue is thick and glossy and the sugar has dissolved. Drop or pipe tablespoons of the meringue onto trays. Bake for 50–60 minutes, until dry to touch. Turn off the oven and open the door. Allow the meringues to cool completely in the oven.

5 Spoon lemon curd into the biscuit cases, top with a meringue and serve.

Mum's poppyseed cake

When my mum makes this cake, everyone raves about it, me included, and until now she has always kept the secret – it starts with packet cake. I don't usually approve of cake mixes, but this recipe is just too good not to share with you.

Serves 8

4 eggs

½ cup caster sugar

2 oranges, rind finely grated

½ cup extra-light olive oil or sunflower oil

1 packet Golden Buttercake mix
   (White Wings brand)

300ml sour cream, lightly beaten

½ cup poppy seeds

Cream cheese frosting

200g cream cheese, softened

1 cup pure icing sugar, sifted

1 teaspoon freshly squeezed
   orange juice

1 Preheat the oven to 180°C no fan/160°C fan-forced. Grease and line a 20cm (base) round cake pan.

2 Using an electric mixer, beat the eggs, sugar and orange rind on high speed for about 5–8 minutes, until thick and pale. Stir in the oil, and then the dry cake mix. ★ Gently fold in the sour cream, then the poppy seeds.

3 Pour the mixture into the cake pan and bake for 50–60 minutes, or until a skewer inserted into the centre comes out clean. (If the cake starts to colour too much, place a piece of foil loosely over the top after 45 minutes.) Stand in the cake pan for 10 minutes before turning onto a wire rack to cool.

4 For the cream cheese frosting, using an electric mixer, beat the cream cheese until light and fluffy. Add the icing sugar 1 spoonful at a time and beat until thick. Stir in the orange juice, then spread over the top and sides of the cake.

★ If the cake mix has clumped together in the packet, break up any lumps with your fingertips before adding it to the egg mixture.

Summer fruit salad

Palm sugar syrup is sensational drizzled over any combination of summer fruits, but lychees, mangoes and watermelon look beautiful together.

Serves 6

4 mangoes, peeled, chopped

12 fresh or canned lychees

¼ seedless watermelon, peeled, chopped

fresh mint leaves & little coconut meringues, optional, to serve (see page 204)

Palm sugar syrup

1 cup chopped palm sugar

²/₃ cup water

1 cup mint leaves

2 limes, rind shredded, juiced

⅓ cup chilled white rum, optional

1 For the palm sugar syrup, combine the sugar, water and mint leaves in a saucepan over medium heat. Cook, stirring occasionally, for 5 minutes, or until the sugar has dissolved. Increase the heat to medium-high and, without stirring, bring the syrup to the boil. Boil gently for 5 minutes, until the syrup reduces slightly. Remove from the heat and set aside to cool to room temperature.

2 Strain the syrup, discarding the mint leaves. Add the lime rind, juice and white rum, if using. Refrigerate or place in the freezer until cold.

3 Combine the mango, lychees and watermelon in a serving bowl and pour over the chilled syrup. Top with mint leaves and serve with little coconut meringues if desired (see page 204).

Strawberry & cream tart

This amazing tart is one of the easiest you will ever make. You can have it on the table within 30 minutes.

Serves 6

500g strawberries, hulled, halved

2 tablespoons pure icing sugar

1 tablespoon liqueur (such as Kahlúa or Grand Marnier), optional

2 sheets frozen ready-rolled puff pastry ♥

1 tablespoon white sugar

250g mascarpone

♥ If you are like me and have discovered Carême frozen pastry, replace the 2 sheets with 1 × 450g packet, rolled out to a 23cm square.

1 Place the strawberries in a bowl, sprinkle over the icing sugar, then drizzle over the liqueur, if using. Toss gently to combine, cover and refrigerate until ready to serve.

2 Meanwhile, preheat the oven and a large flat tray to 200°C fan-forced. Place 1 pastry sheet on a piece of baking paper. Top with the second sheet, then sprinkle the top sheet with the white sugar.

3 Being careful not to cut all the way through, use a small sharp knife to cut a 2cm-thick border around all four of the pastry edges. Place a 19cm square piece of baking paper in the centre of the pastry (inside the border), then place a 19cm square (base) cake pan on top. ★ Half fill the pan with rice. Using the paper, quickly lift the pastry onto the hot tray and bake for 15 minutes, or until the edges are light golden. Remove the cake pan and the piece of baking paper under it and bake for a further 8–10 minutes, until crisp and cooked through. Set aside to cool on the tray.

4 Keeping within the border, spoon the mascarpone evenly over the pastry base. Spoon over the strawberries and any syrup in the bowl. Serve.

★ The pan helps to press down and condense the centre of the tart, which makes the base crisp and also allows the borders to rise higher.

Choc honeycomb crisps with affogato

Some nights you want to serve up something sweet at the end of meal; on others, I find myself thinking late in the evening that I could just do with a little something. These honeycomb crisps fit both scenarios. Keep them in an airtight container in the back of the fridge for up to a month.

Makes 12 honeycomb crisps & 2 affogatto

200g good-quality dark, milk or white chocolate

¼ cup chocolate hazelnut spread (such as Nutella)

2 cups rice bubbles

35g chocolate-coated honeycomb, finely chopped ♥

cocoa powder, for sprinkling, optional

Affogatto

½ cup freshly brewed double-strength espresso

2 scoops vanilla ice-cream

1 Break the chocolate into even pieces and place into a clean, dry, heat-proof and microwave-safe bowl. Microwave, uncovered, in 1 minute bursts on High/100%, stirring every minute with a metal spoon until melted and smooth. Stir in the hazelnut spread.

2 Place the rice bubbles in a snap lock bag and seal. Use a rolling pin or the palm of your hand to crush the rice bubbles. Add to the chocolate mixture with the honeycomb and stir until well combined.

3 Line a flat baking tray with baking paper. Spread the mixture as thin as possible over the tray – it should be about 20cm × 30cm. Refrigerate until firm, then cut or break into pieces.

4 For the affogato, pour the espresso into 2 heat-proof glasses. Add 1 scoop of ice-cream to each glass and serve with the honeycomb crisps.

♥ You can replace the honeycomb with Peppermint Crisp or Crunchie bars or crushed Maltesers.

Lemon blueberry friends

Years back everyone was making friends, and I got to the stage where I couldn't look at another one, but I am asked all the time for a good recipe. When I made these again for this book I remembered why they were and still are so easy to eat. The secret is to make them two or three days before you serve them – standing allows them to mellow, so they're not sickly sweet.

Makes 12

180g butter, chopped
1²/₃ cups pure icing sugar
½ cup plain flour
1 cup ground almonds ★
5 small eggs, separated ♥
1 lemon, rind finely grated
1 cup fresh or frozen blueberries
pure icing sugar, to serve

★ The fresher the ground almonds, the better the friands.

♥ These friands are best made using the whites from small 55g eggs, rather than the standard 59g eggs.

1 Preheat the oven to 230°C no fan/220°C fan-forced. Lightly grease a 12-hole, ⅓-cup capacity muffin pan and line the base of each hole with a round of baking paper or a paper friand case.

2 Melt the butter in a small saucepan over medium-high heat until it turns light golden in colour. Set aside to cool slightly.

3 Sift the icing sugar and flour together in a large bowl and stir in the almonds. Add the egg whites and lemon rind and mix well. Strain the butter into the mixture and stir gently until just combined. Pour into the muffin holes until almost full. Poke 3–4 blueberries into the top of each friand.

4 Bake for 5 minutes. Reduce oven to 200°C no fan/190°C fan-forced and bake for a further 10–15 minutes, or until golden. When cooked, a skewer inserted into the centre should come out clean. Allow to stand for 5 minutes in the pan, then turn out onto a wire rack to cool. Dust generously with icing sugar to serve.

Toffee fruit with cheesecake ice-cream

Serves 4

8 freestone peaches, nectarines or plums,
   halved, stones removed
1 cup white sugar

Cheesecake ice-cream
1 litre good-quality vanilla ice-cream
500g cream cheese, softened, chopped
½ cup caster sugar
1 teaspoon vanilla bean paste
⅔ cup thickened cream

1 For the cheesecake ice-cream, spoon the ice-cream into a large mixing bowl. Set aside at room temperature for 10–20 minutes to soften slightly. Meanwhile, using an electric mixer, beat the cream cheese, caster sugar and vanilla together until smooth and creamy. Pour in the thickened cream and beat until just combined.

2 Stir the cream cheese mixture into the vanilla ice-cream until well combined. Pour into a 5-cup capacity airtight container ♥ and place a piece of baking paper right onto the surface. Cover with plastic wrap, then secure with a tight-fitting lid or wrap tightly in foil and freeze overnight.

3 Line a tray with baking paper. Place the fruit, cut side up, on the tray.

4 Pour the sugar into a clean, dry, medium non-stick frying pan. Place over medium heat and cook, stirring occasionally with a wooden spoon, until the sugar melts and turns deep golden. Remove from the heat and pour the toffee mixture over the fruit. Set aside for 10 minutes to allow the toffee to set and cool. ★ Serve with scoops of cheesecake ice-cream.

♥ To prevent freezer burn, it's important to store the ice-cream in a container only just large enough to hold it, though allowing it just a little room to expand when it freezes. Once it's frozen, press a piece of baking paper right down onto the surface to prevent ice crystals forming.

★ You can make the fruit in advance, if you like, and refrigerate it. The crisp toffee will melt to a sweet syrup, which is just as delicious.

Mascarpone figs with real caramel sauce

Fresh figs are the most seductive fruit on the planet. They come in and out of season quickly, so keep an eye out for them. If you're watching the kilojoules, replace the mascarpone with Greek yoghurt or ricotta.

Serves 4
½ cup pistachio kernels
1 teaspoon vanilla bean paste
250g mascarpone
12 small or 8 large fresh figs

Real caramel sauce ★
1½ cups white sugar
300ml thickened cream

★ The caramel will keep for
3 months in the fridge in a clean,
sterilised, airtight jar.

1 Preheat the oven to 180°C fan-forced. Place the pistachio kernels on a baking tray and cook for 8 minutes, or until toasted. Set aside to cool, then roughly chop. Fold the nuts and vanilla gently through the mascarpone. Cover and refrigerate until ready to serve.

2 For the real caramel sauce, pour the sugar into a small, clean, dry, non-stick frying pan over medium heat. Cook, stirring occasionally with a wooden spoon, until the sugar melts and turns deep golden. Remove from the heat and carefully pour in the cream. (The sugar will spit a little and turn to toffee.) Return the pan to medium-high heat and cook, stirring constantly, for 5–8 minutes, until the toffee dissolves and the sauce is smooth. Simmer gently for 5 minutes, without stirring, to thicken slightly.

3 Cut a cross in the figs and gently ease open. Spoon in the mascarpone mixture. Arrange on a serving plate and spoon over the warm caramel sauce to serve.

Pavlova parfait

The first time I made this dessert was when I went to slide a pavlova onto a serving plate and it cracked and broke. Not wanting to take an imperfect dish to a friend's place I went to plan B and created this parfait instead. It was a smash hit – pardon the pun!

Serves 6

300ml thickened cream
2 tablespoons caster sugar
1 teaspoon vanilla extract
3 small mangoes, peeled, chopped
4 passionfruit, halved

Pavlova

3 egg whites, at room temperature
pinch cream of tartar
¾ cup caster sugar
2 teaspoons cornflour
½ teaspoon vanilla extract
1 teaspoon freshly squeezed lemon juice

1 Preheat the oven to 130°C no fan/120°C fan-forced. Draw a 20cm circle on a piece of baking paper and use to line a lightly greased flat baking tray, pencil mark facing down.

2 For the pavlova, using an electric mixer, beat the egg whites and cream of tartar in a large, clean, dry bowl until firm peaks just start to form. Gradually add the sugar, 1 spoonful at a time, beating to dissolve the sugar before adding the next spoonful. Once all the sugar is added, fold in the cornflour, vanilla and lemon juice.

3 Spoon the pavlova mixture onto the tray, using the circle on the paper as a guide. Reduce the oven temperature to 110°C no fan/100°C fan-forced. Bake for 1 hour, or until the pavlova is crisp on the outside and a skewer inserted in the centre comes out clean. Turn the oven off, open the oven door slightly and allow the pavlova to cool for 2–3 hours.

4 Whip the cream in a large bowl until thick. Fold in the sugar and vanilla. ★ Break the pavlova into chunks and fold into the cream. Spoon half the mango and passionfruit pulp over the base of 6 chilled serving glasses or 1 × 6-cup capacity bowl. Top with the pavlova cream mixture, then the remaining mango and passionfruit. Serve.

★ This dessert is best assembled no more than an hour before serving, but the pavlova and fruit can be prepared up to 4 hours ahead.

Brown sugar pears with coconut custard

Fans of Ready Steady Cook *will know Pete Everett, the host, is one of my dearest friends, and he loves custard. Not just any custard – one that's made from eggs, milk and cream. This is for him, and the rest of us who love custard with everything.*

Serves 4

4 firm beurre bosc pears, quartered,
   core removed
3 tablespoons brown sugar
olive oil cooking spray

Coconut custard
200ml coconut cream
1 cup milk
4 egg yolks
2 tablespoons vanilla sugar ★
½ teaspoon vanilla bean paste
1 teaspoon cornflour

★ To make vanilla sugar, place vanilla beans in an airtight jar and fill it with caster sugar. Seal and set aside for at least a week before using it. Keep topping up with sugar and vanilla beans as required.

1 Place a roasting pan in the oven and preheat the oven and pan to 250°C fan-forced.

2 Place the pears on a large plate, sprinkle over the sugar and turn to coat. The sugar will start to dissolve. Remove the hot pan from the oven and spray lightly with oil. Add the pears and all the sugar and any juices on the plate to the hot pan. Roast for 10 minutes, turning the pears once or twice, until golden and just tender. Turn the oven off and allow the pears to stand in the oven for 5 minutes.

3 Meanwhile, for the coconut custard, combine the coconut cream and the milk in a heavy-based saucepan over medium-low heat. Cook, stirring often, for 10 minutes, or until mixture is hot. Using an electric mixer, beat the egg yolks, vanilla sugar, vanilla bean paste and cornflour until pale. Add the warm cream mixture and beat on low speed to combine. Pour the mixture back into the saucepan and cook over a low heat, stirring constantly, for 10–15 minutes, or until the custard thickens and coats the wooden spoon. Do not boil.

4 Serve the brown sugar pears with the coconut custard.

Mango pan pudding

In over 650 episodes of Ready Steady Cook *there was only one time I was really confident that I would win. It was when I made a smaller version of this pudding. (Okay, it had nothing to do with the pudding – my guest chef was from* Bondi Rescue *and the audience was full of schoolgirls. But it does taste amazing!)*

Serves 4

80g butter, softened

½ cup caster sugar

1 egg

½ cup shredded coconut

¾ cup self-raising flour, sifted

⅓ cup sour cream

1 large firm ripe mango, peeled, sliced

3 teaspoons white sugar ♥

cheesecake ice-cream, to serve
  (see page 90)

♥ The white sugar helps the mango hold its shape during cooking.

1 Preheat the oven to 180°C fan-forced. Lightly grease a 16cm (base), 20cm (top) non-stick ovenproof frying pan. Line the base with a round of baking paper.

2 Using an electric mixer, beat the butter and caster sugar until pale and creamy. Add the egg and beat until well combined. Fold through the coconut and flour, and then the sour cream.

3 Place the lined pan over a medium heat for 2–3 minutes, until warm. Spread the pudding mixture over the base of the warm pan. Cook for 3 minutes. Arrange the sliced mango over the top of the pudding and sprinkle with white sugar.

4 Transfer the pudding to the oven and bake for 25–30 minutes, or until a skewer inserted into the centre comes out clean. Stand for 5 minutes in the pan before serving with cheesecake ice-cream.

Chocolate self-saucing pudding

This is a family favourite. When we all get together I triple this recipe, and it still only takes 35 minutes to cook. The secret to the right balance of pudding to sauce is the depth of the dish.

Serves 4

100g good-quality dark chocolate, chopped
50g butter, chopped
½ cup milk
¾ cup self-raising flour, sifted
¼ cup brown sugar
2 tablespoons cocoa powder
cream or vanilla ice-cream, to serve

Topping

¾ cup brown sugar
2 tablespoons cocoa powder
1½ cups boiling water

1 Preheat the oven to 180°C fan-forced. Combine the chocolate, butter and milk in a heat-proof microwave-safe bowl. Microwave, uncovered, on High/100% for 1–2 minutes, stirring every minute with a metal spoon until melted and smooth.

2 Combine the flour, brown sugar and cocoa powder in a bowl. Stir in the chocolate mixture and mix well. Spoon into a lightly greased 6-cup capacity, 5cm-deep, 15cm × 25cm ovenproof dish.

3 For the topping, combine the brown sugar and cocoa in a bowl, then sprinkle over the pudding mixture. Pour the boiling water slowly over the topping. Place the dish on a tray and bake for 30–35 minutes, until a skewer inserted into the centre of the pudding comes out clean.

4 Serve within 10 minutes of removing from oven. otherwise the pudding starts to absorb the sauce. (It's still yummy, but there's not as much sauce to go around.) Serve with cream or ice-cream.

Microwave rhubarb & vanilla jam

The consistency of this jam is like stewed fruit . . . But as my dear friend Pete Everett said, 'It's too good to just have on toast!' He served large spoonfuls over bowls of warm rice pudding, to guests who were blown away!

Makes 2½ cups
2 bunches rhubarb (about 600g each)
1 large lemon, juiced
2 cups white or raw sugar
2 vanilla beans, halved
crumpets, toasted to serve

1 Remove and discard the tops and leaves of the rhubarb. Trim 2cm off the base of each stalk and wash the stems well, leaving water clinging. Cut the rhubarb into 4cm lengths and place in a large, microwave-safe, heat-proof bowl. Cover with 2 layers of plastic wrap and microwave for 6–8 minutes on High/100%, or until pulpy.

2 Carefully remove the plastic wrap and stir the rhubarb. Stir in the lemon juice and sugar. Scrape the soft seeds from the vanilla bean halves and add the seeds and beans to the bowl. Microwave, uncovered, for 15–18 minutes on High/100%, stirring every 5 minutes, until thick and jam-like.

3 Ladle the hot jam into hot sterilised jars, seal and label. ♥ Once opened, the jam will keep for 3 months in the fridge.

♥ To sterilise jars, preheat the oven to 110°C fan-forced. Wash the jars and lids in hot soapy water, then rinse. Place the jars in a large saucepan covered with cold water and bring to the boil over high heat. Boil gently for 10 minutes, then place the jars and lids upside down on a baking tray lined with a clean tea towel. Transfer to the oven for 15 minutes. Always bottle hot jam or sauces into hot jars and cooled jam and sauces into cold jars.

Rhubarb &
Vanilla bean
Jam

Spiced
fruit & nut
nibble mix

Spiced fruit & nut nibble mix

I think 'be prepared' was the Girl Guides (or Brownies) motto. When I leave the house I always have a large bottle of water and, more often than not, a container of this mix in my handbag. Nuts are a good source of protein and keep you feeling full – but don't be tempted to eat more than a small handful at a time. Too much of a good thing is bad for you.

Makes 6 cups

2 egg whites
2 tablespoons caster sugar
3 teaspoons ground cumin
3 teaspoons ground coriander
2 teaspoons garam masala
1 teaspoon ground fennel seeds
1 teaspoon ground turmeric
½ teaspoon ground cinnamon
¼ teaspoon cayenne pepper
5 cups mixed nuts
100g packet fried noodles
½ cup mixed seeds
   (such as pepita & sunflower)
2 tablespoons sesame seeds
1 cup raisins

1 Preheat the oven to 180°C fan-forced. Line a large shallow roasting pan with baking paper.

2 Using a hand beater, beat the egg whites in a clean, dry, medium bowl to soft peaks. Add the sugar a little at a time, beating constantly until it has dissolved. Combine all the spices in a bowl, then gently stir into the egg white mixture to combine.

3 Combine the nuts, noodles, mixed seeds and sesame seeds in a large bowl. Add the spice mixture and stir to coat. Spread the mixture into the roasting pan.

4 Bake, stirring every 5 minutes ♥, for 25–30 minutes, or until the nuts are toasted and feel dry. Set aside to cool completely. Carefully break up the nut mix and add the raisins, then spoon into clean airtight jars. The nibble mix will keep for 2 months.

♥ It is really important to stir, otherwise the coating will fall off the nuts when they cool.

Weekend feasts

As the working week comes to an end, on our rare days off, or when holidays loom, we allow ourselves to take the foot off the pedal, release the pressure valve and find a little more time for what's important. The following recipes take just a tiny bit longer to cook or prepare, but they still have my characteristic approach — they're sensible and easy to follow, and the results are fresh, stylish and full of flavour.

Time to cook

While the recipes in this chapter are perfect for leisurely weekend fare, you shouldn't discount them for midweek meals. Running around all over town looking for something new isn't how I like to spend my days off, so the ingredients I call for are all familiar and easy to find. The steps and techniques have also been kept simple. As you create, serve and enjoy these dishes, you will experience a depth of flavour well worth that little bit of extra time and effort you've put in.

Boston-style baked beans

My introduction to TV cooking goes back to What's Cooking with Gabriel Gaté, *but the real stars of the show were the chef (Phil) and home ec (Julie), who worked behind the scenes. They wrote, tested and developed almost all the recipes seen on air. Plenty of learning and experimenting happened in Phil's kitchen – and that's where I tasted the best baked beans I have ever eaten.*

Serves 6–8 as a main meal

2 cups dried haricot or white navy beans

450g bacon bones

1 tablespoon extra-virgin olive oil

2 brown onions, diced

140g tub tomato paste

1 tablespoon French mustard

2 tablespoons brown sugar

2 tablespoons molasses

1 tablespoon Worcestershire sauce

chopped flat-leaf parsley, to serve

hot buttered toast, to serve

1 Place the beans in a large bowl, then cover with 2 litres of cold water and stand for 5 minutes. Drain and repeat twice. Cover again with water, then set aside for 24 hours to soak. (Alternatively, to speed up the process, after rinsing 3 times, tip the beans into a large saucepan, cover with cold water and bring to the boil. Boil for 5 minutes, then remove from the heat and set aside for 1½ hours in the liquid.)

2 Drain and rinse the beans well, tip into a large saucepan and cover with cold water. Place over medium heat and bring to a simmer. Simmer gently for 30–45 minutes, or until the beans are just tender. Drain well. ♥

3 Place the bacon bones in a large saucepan, cover with 4 cups of cold water and bring to the boil over medium-high heat. Reduce the heat to medium and simmer, uncovered, for 40 minutes.

4 Meanwhile, heat the oil in a frying pan over medium heat, add the onion and cook for 4 minutes, until soft. Add the tomato paste and cook for 1 minute. Remove from the heat and stir in the mustard, brown sugar, molasses and Worcestershire sauce.

5 Strain the bacon bones from the stock, place the bones on a board and pour 3 cups of the stock back into the saucepan. Add the beans and onion mixture to the stock. Remove the bacon meat from the bones and roughly chop. Discard the bones and add the meat to the bean mixture. Simmer over medium-low heat for 20–30 minutes, or until thickened. Taste, then season with salt and pepper. Sprinkle with parsley and serve with hot buttered toast.

♥ To speed things up, you can use 4 cups of canned cannellini beans instead of dried beans. Start from the end of step 2, making sure the beans are well rinsed.

Cheese & basil pull-apart

The house fills with the most amazing aroma as you bake this easy, yeast-free pull-apart. It's best eaten the day it's made – hot or cold. Serve it with soup or dips, or for brunch topped with cream cheese and smoked salmon. It's also perfect picnic fare (see the Portable Picnic menu on page 231).

Serves 6–8

3½ cups self-raising flour, sifted

40g parmesan, finely grated

300ml thickened cream

1–1¼ cups milk

2 tablespoons extra-virgin olive oil

2 cups finely shredded basil leaves

½ cup flat-leaf parsley, chopped

150g feta, crumbled

1 teaspoon sea salt flakes

1 Preheat the oven to 220°C fan-forced. Lightly grease a 7cm-deep, 10cm × 20cm loaf pan and line the base only with baking paper.

2 Combine the flour and parmesan in a large bowl. Add the cream, 1 cup of milk and 1 tablespoon of oil and stir with a flat-bladed knife to form a soft dough, adding more milk if necessary. Turn onto a lightly floured surface and knead gently until the dough comes together.

3 Combine the basil, parsley and feta in a bowl. Divide the dough into 7 even portions. Roll each portion into a 10cm × 18cm rectangle. Spread the basil mixture evenly over each portion. Roll up each rectangle, starting from the long edge, to enclose filling. Cut in half crossways and place side by side in the pan, cut side down.

4 Brush the top of the loaf with the remaining oil and sprinkle with sea salt flakes. Bake for 38–40 minutes, or until golden and cooked through. Serve warm or at room temperature.

Corn & haloumi fritters with eggplant dip

Good reliable fritter recipes are hard to find. My secret is squeezing the moisture from the potato in a clean tea towel.

Serves 12

400g (2 medium) sebago potatoes, peeled

3 corncobs, husks & silk removed

125g haloumi, grated

¼ cup flat-leaf parsley, chopped

2 tablespoons self-raising flour

2 tablespoons plain flour

2 eggs, lightly whisked

olive oil, for shallow-frying

Eggplant dip

2 medium eggplants

6 garlic cloves, skin on

4 green onions, chopped

2 tablespoons organic tahini

2 tablespoons extra-virgin olive oil

½ lemon, juiced

⅓ cup Greek yoghurt

1 tablespoon sesame seeds, toasted

1 For the eggplant dip, preheat the oven to 200°C fan-forced. Pierce each eggplant 6 times with a fork and place in a roasting pan with the garlic. Roast for 40 minutes, or until the eggplants are soft and almost collapsed. Cut the eggplants in half lengthways and scoop the warm flesh into a food processor. Squeeze the roasted garlic flesh from the skins into the processor. Add the green onions, tahini, olive oil and lemon juice and process until smooth. Transfer to a bowl and stir in the yoghurt and sesame seeds. Season with salt and pepper, transfer to an airtight container and refrigerate until ready to serve.

2 Coarsely grate the potato onto a clean tea towel. Gather the tea towel together and squeeze to remove all the moisture from the potato. Transfer the dry potato to a bowl. Slice the corn kernels from the cob and add to the potato with the haloumi and parsley.

3 Sift the flours together in a large bowl, add the egg and stir until smooth. Stir in the corn mixture and season with salt and pepper.

4 Pour enough oil into a large non-stick frying pan to cover the base and heat over medium heat until hot. Drop heaped spoonfuls of the mixture into the pan and cook for 4–5 minutes on each side, or until golden and cooked through. Transfer to a wire rack over a tray lined with paper towel, then keep warm in the oven at 150°C while cooking the remaining fritters. Serve warm or cold with the eggplant dip.

Lime & ginger marmalade glazed vegetables

Serves 6 as side dish

2 parsnips, peeled

2 carrots, peeled

2 turnips, peeled

3 medium beetroot, trimmed, scrubbed

2 tablespoons olive oil

2 garlic cloves, thinly sliced

2 tablespoons lime & ginger marmalade

2 tablespoons maple syrup

1 tablespoon balsamic vinegar

1 Preheat the oven to 220°C fan-forced. Cut parsnips and carrot in half lengthways, remove the core then cut into chunks, Cut the turnips and beetroot into thick wedges. Arrange all the vegetables in a large roasting pan lined with baking paper.

2 Heat oil in a small saucepan over medium heat. Add garlic and cook 1 minute, until aromatic. Add the marmalade, maple syrup and balsamic vinegar, cook stirring occasionally for 3 minutes, until marmalade is melted and glaze hot.

3 Pour the hot glaze over the vegetables and toss gently to coat. Roast for 45–50 minutes, turning occasionally, until golden and crisp. Season with salt and pepper and serve with roadhouse steak with onion rings (see page 56).

Quiche lorraine

I am a quiche lover! Rolling the pastry into tins, preventing shrinkage and baking properly are all things people tell me they are not confident doing, so I created this recipe. It's seriously delicious served warm with dressed baby spinach leaves for dinner or at room temperature for lunch or on a picnic.

Serves 4

50g parmesan, finely grated
275g piece smoked ham, diced
4 green onions, thinly sliced
½ cup thickened cream
4 eggs ♥

Cornmeal pastry

1¼ cups plain flour
⅓ cup cornmeal ★
125g butter, chilled, cubed
2-3 tablespoons chilled water

♥ This recipe only requires the yolks, but it is best to separate them one at a time as needed in step 3. Use the leftover whites to make pavlova parfait (see page 94).

★ Cornmeal is sometimes labelled polenta.

1 For the cornmeal pastry, place the flour and cornmeal in a food processor and pulse to combine. Add the butter and process until the mixture resembles coarse breadcrumbs. Add 2 tablespoons of water and process until the pastry comes together, adding more water if necessary. Turn onto a lightly floured surface and knead lightly until smooth. Shape into a rectangle. If it's a warm day, wrap in greaseproof paper and refrigerate for 20 minutes, until firm enough to roll out.

2 Preheat the oven and a large flat baking tray to 200°C fan-forced. Roll the pastry out between 2 sheets of baking paper to form a 24cm × 36cm rectangle. Remove the top sheet of baking paper.

3 Sprinkle three-quarters of the parmesan over the pastry, leaving a 2cm border around all four edges. Top with the ham and green onions. Fold the pastry border over the ham, leaving the centre of the quiche exposed. Carefully drizzle the cream over the filling. Make a small indentation in one end of the filling. Separate 1 egg and drop the yolk into the indentation. Repeat using the remaining 3 yolks, spacing them evenly over the filling. Brush the top of the pastry with water and sprinkle over the remaining parmesan. Season with salt and pepper.

4 Using the baking paper, carefully lift the quiche onto the hot tray and bake for 30–35 minutes, or until the pastry is golden and crisp. Set aside on the tray for 10 minutes. Cut into pieces and serve.

Balsamic-glazed roasted tomatoes

I used to be able to buy these tomatoes in a little deli, but the shop has since closed. After many days of testing at home, I mastered the recipe. They are amazing on an antipasto plate, sandwiches, pizzas or tossed in a salad. They keep for 3 months in airtight jar in the fridge.

Makes 20

1kg (about 10 medium) Roma tomatoes

2 teaspoons sea salt flakes

6 garlic cloves, thinly sliced

2 teaspoons dried oregano

extra-virgin olive oil

prosciutto, buffalo mozzarella, crusty
   bread & eggplant dip (see page 115),
   to serve

Balsamic glaze

¼ cup white sugar

¼ cup balsamic vinegar

1 tablespoon warm water

1 Slice the tomatoes in half horizontally and scoop out most of the seeds. Crush the sea salt flakes between your fingers and sprinkle over the cut side of the tomatoes. Place cut side down on a wire rack over a baking tray, cover with a clean tea towel and set aside for 1 hour.

2 Preheat the oven to 120°C fan-forced. Place the tomatoes cut side up in a lightly greased baking dish. Top each with slices of garlic and sprinkle with oregano. Drizzle with a little olive oil and roast for 3 hours, or until collapsed and semi-dried.

3 For the balsamic glaze, pour the sugar into a small non-stick frying pan and place over medium- high heat. Cook for 3–4 minutes, stirring and tilting the pan occasionally, until the sugar turns a deep golden colour. Remove from the heat and carefully add the balsamic vinegar (the mixture will spit). Return the pan to the heat, add water and stir over medium heat until the glaze is smooth.

4 Pour the hot balsamic glaze over the tomatoes and return to the oven to roast for a further 30 minutes. Set aside to cool completely.

5 Add to a salad or serve with prosciutto, buffalo mozzarella, crusty bread and eggplant dip.

Fold-over barbecue pizza

One of the most popular recipes in my first book, Fast, Fresh & Fabulous, *is the Turkish gozleme – I get emails from people all the time about how much they love them. Well, this is next step – a quick, easy, yeast version! For non-vegetarians, add chopped spicy salami.*

Makes 4

1 cup warm water

3 teaspoons instant dried yeast

1 teaspoon caster sugar

¼ cup extra-virgin olive oil

3 cups plain flour

1 garlic clove, crushed

½ cup tomato passata (see below)

½ cup semi-dried tomatoes, chopped

200g roasted red capsicum, chopped
  (see page 46)

200g char-grilled eggplant, chopped

⅓ cup basil leaves, shredded

250g mozzarella, thinly sliced

200g ricotta, crumbled

Tomato passata ♥

2 tablespoons olive oil

1 small brown onion, finely chopped

2 large garlic cloves, crushed

800g can whole peeled tomatoes

pinch white sugar

1½ teaspoons dried oregano

♥ This tomato passata recipe makes 2½ cups. It will keep in a sterilised jar in the fridge for up to 2 months.

1 For the tomato passata, heat the oil in a saucepan over medium heat. Add the onion and garlic and cook for 5 minutes, or until the onion is soft. Add the tomatoes, sugar and a good pinch of salt and plenty of freshly ground black pepper. Cook, breaking up the tomatoes with a wooden spoon, for 10 minutes, or until the sauce comes to the boil. Reduce the heat to medium-low and simmer for 15 minutes. Spoon into a food processor and process until almost smooth. Stir the oregano into the warm sauce, taste and adjust the salt and pepper. Ladle the hot sauce into hot sterilised jars, seal and label.

2 Combine the warm water, yeast, sugar, a pinch of salt and 1½ tablespoons of oil in a large bowl. Add the flour and mix well. Knead on a lightly floured surface for 8 minutes, until elastic. Cover and set aside for 15 minutes. Combine the remaining oil and garlic in a small bowl.

3 Preheat a flat barbecue plate on high heat. Cut the dough into 4 pieces and roll each piece out to a rectangle roughly 20cm × 30cm. Spread 2 tablespoons of the passata evenly over each piece of dough. Top half of each piece of dough with tomato, capsicum, eggplant, basil, mozzarella and ricotta. Fold the un-topped dough over the filling and roll the edges to seal.

4 Brush both sides of the pizzas lightly with the garlic oil. Reduce the barbecue heat to medium, place the pizzas on the plate and close the hood. Barbecue for 5–7 minutes on each side, until golden and crisp. Cut into pieces and serve.

Silverbeet & ricotta gnocchi

Making gnocchi is way down on most people's list of what to cook. This used to be the case for me too, but after spending three days in the kitchen testing and testing, trying to find a truly foolproof method, I am converted. I know you will love this – it comes with a money-back guarantee.

Serves 4

500g ricotta
100g (5 large stalks) silverbeet
40g parmesan, finely grated
2 egg yolks
¾–1 cup plain flour
extra plain flour, for dusting
60g unsalted butter, chopped
small basil leaves & finely grated
  parmesan, to serve

★ Before you roll and cut the rest, bring a small saucepan of salted water to the boil, add 2–3 gnocchi and cook for 1–2 minutes. If they don't fall apart when cooked, continue to cut and shape the remaining gnocchi. If they do fall apart, add a little more flour to the dough and repeat.

1 Place the ricotta in a sieve over a bowl, cover and refrigerate for 2 hours to allow excess moisture to drain. Cut the silverbeet leaves from the stems. Wash and dry the leaves, then finely shred and place on a microwave-safe plate. Cover with paper towel and microwave for 30 seconds on High/100%. Working quickly, spread the silverbeet onto a wire rack to cool, then transfer to a large bowl.

2 Place the ricotta, parmesan and egg yolks in a food processor and process until as smooth as possible (a little texture is fine). Add to the silverbeet and stir to combine. Gradually add the flour ¼ cup at a time, stirring to form a dough the consistency of thick mashed potatoes. You may not need all of the flour (and the less you use, the lighter the gnocchi will be). Divide the dough into 4 pieces.

3 Generously dust the bench and your hands with flour, then roll one piece of the dough into a 3cm-thick, 24cm-long log. Cut into 1½–2cm lengths with a floured knife. ★ Repeat with the remaining mixture. Using lightly floured hands, re-roll the cut pieces into gnocchi shapes.

4 Bring a large saucepan of salted water to boil over high heat. Carefully add one-quarter of the gnocchi, one at a time, into the water. Reduce the heat if necessary – the water should be bubbling, but not rapidly boiling. Cook, uncovered, for 2 minutes, or until most of the gnocchi float to the top. Use a slotted spoon to transfer the gnocchi to a lightly greased ovenproof dish. Cover with foil to keep warm. Return the water to the boil and repeat with the remaining gnocchi in 3 more batches.

5 Preheat the grill on medium-high. Melt the butter in a frying pan over medium heat for 2 minutes, or until it turns a light brown. Pour the butter over the warm gnocchi. Place under a hot grill and cook for 2 minutes, until the edges of the gnocchi begin to turn light golden. Spoon into shallow bowls and top with the basil and extra parmesan. Season well with salt and pepper and serve.

Buttermilk chicken

This is better than any take-out – it's half the price and way less kilojoules (so you can enjoy dessert without guilt). It's also perfect lunch box and picnic food. I have a feeling this will quickly become part of your repertoire.

Serves 4–6

1 cup buttermilk

2 teaspoons Tabasco sauce

8 pieces chicken on bone
  (such as thigh cutlets, marylands, legs)

1½ cups plain flour

2 teaspoons baking powder

2 teaspoons sea salt flakes

3 teaspoons sweet paprika

2 tablespoons sesame seeds

olive oil cooking spray

1 Combine the buttermilk and Tabasco in a large snap lock bag. Add the chicken and massage to coat. Secure the bag and refrigerate for minimum 2 hours (overnight is best).

2 Preheat the oven to 220°C fan-forced. Line a baking tray with baking paper. Combine the flour, baking powder, salt, paprika and sesame seeds in another large snap lock bag and shake to combine. Add one chicken piece at a time to the bag and shake to coat. Place the chicken on the tray and spray lightly with olive oil.

3 Roast the chicken for 45 minutes, or until golden, crisp and cooked through. Serve with carrot salad (see page 150).

Thai chicken, mango & coconut salad

This is a sensational light dinner for those warm balmy summer evenings, and also doubles as a starter when piled onto the crispy wontons. Take any leftovers for lunch.

Serves 4

1 tablespoon olive oil

3 chicken breast fillets, trimmed

12 wonton wrappers

peanut oil, for deep-frying

2 green mangoes ★

200g snow peas, topped

2 Lebanese cucumbers, halved
　lengthways, seeds removed

4 green onions, thinly sliced

1½ cups bean sprouts, trimmed

⅔ cup small mint leaves

¾ cup shredded coconut, toasted

Dressing

¼ cup coconut milk

1 garlic clove, crushed

2 tablespoons chilli jam or
　sweet chilli sauce

1 lime, juiced

1 teaspoon brown sugar

1 Preheat the oven to 180°C fan-forced. Heat a large non-stick frying pan over high heat until hot. Add the oil and swirl to coat the base. Add the chicken breast fillets and cook for 2 minutes on each side, or until light golden. Transfer the pan to the oven and roast for 5–8 minutes, or until just cooked through. Remove from the oven, cover loosely with foil and stand for 10 minutes.

2 Deep-fry the wonton wrappers one at a time in peanut oil until golden and crisp, then drain on a wire rack and set aside to cool.

3 Meanwhile, peel and thinly slice the mango with a julienne peeler and place in a bowl. Cut the snow peas and cucumber into thin strips and add to the mango. Add the green onions, bean sprouts, mint and coconut and toss to combine. Shred the warm chicken and add to the salad.

4 To make the dressing, combine all the ingredients in a screw-top jar and shake.

5 Pour the dressing over the salad just before serving and toss gently. Top with wonton chips and serve.

★ Green mangoes are available from Asian grocery stores and some greengrocers. If you don't have an Asian grocer nearby, large firm mangoes such as R2E2 (available November to February) or Calypso (September to March) are equally as good. Green papaya is a suitable substitute when mangoes are not available.

Twice-cooked soy chicken

While studying at TAFE, one of my favourite classes was cultural cooking, where we learnt the history and cooking techniques of many different cuisines. This recipe stuck. It's easy, and tastes every bit as good as the restaurant version.

Serves 4

1.5kg whole chicken, cleaned

4 cups water

2 cups Shaoxing Chinese cooking wine

1 cup dark soy sauce

1 cup Chinese rock sugar or
  brown sugar

2 stems lemongrass, bruised

3 small fresh red chillies, halved

5cm piece ginger, thinly sliced

2 cinnamon sticks

1 mandarin

2 tablespoons honey

1 teaspoon sesame oil

steamed choy sum & jasmine rice,
  to serve

1 Cut the chicken in half through the breast bone, then turn it over on a board and press hard on the backbone to flatten the chicken. Cut down either side of the backbone, then remove and discard the backbone. Tuck wings under.

2 Combine the water, cooking wine, soy, sugar, lemongrass, chillies, ginger and cinnamon sticks in a medium-large wok or large saucepan. Peel and juice the mandarin and add the peel and juice to the wok. Place over medium-high heat and bring to a simmer, stirring to dissolve the sugar.

3 Reduce the heat to low and add the chicken halves, skin side down. Cover and simmer gently for 30 minutes. Remove from the heat and stand in the poaching liquid for another hour. Remove the chicken halves carefully and reserve 1 cup of the cooking liquid. ♥

4 Pour the reserved cooking liquid into a saucepan and bring to the boil over high heat. Boil gently for 8–10 minutes, until reduced by half. Remove from the heat and stir in the honey and sesame oil. Set aside to cool.

5 Preheat the oven to 200°C fan-forced. Place the chicken halves skin side up in a roasting pan lined with baking paper. Spoon over the honey soy mixture. Roast for 20 minutes, until crisp and cooked through, basting occasionally with the honey soy mixture as it thickens on the base of the pan. Cut the chicken halves into pieces and serve with choy sum and rice.

♥ Pour the remaining cooking liquid into a saucepan and bring it to the boil. Boil for 5 minutes and then set it aside to cool. Strain it into a container or freezer bag and freeze for the next time you make this dish.

Greek-inspired cabbage rolls

Cabbage rolls are under-rated. These are light enough to enjoy all year round and, best of all, they can be made in advance, as they reheat beautifully.

Makes 8

400g lamb mince
100g ricotta
125g feta, crumbled
1 cup basil leaves, shredded
1 lemon, rind finely grated, juiced
2 tablespoons pine nuts, toasted, chopped
1 large Chinese cabbage
16 thin slices spicy pancetta
2 cups chicken stock

1 Preheat the oven to 170°C fan-forced. Combine the lamb mince, ricotta, feta, basil, lemon rind, juice and pine nuts in a large bowl and season with salt and pepper. Mix with your hands until well combined. Separate the cabbage leaves, then choose 8 large ones and wash well.

2 Bring a large saucepan of salted water to the boil. Add the cabbage leaves, 2–3 at a time, and cook for 1 minute, until wilted and bright green. Refresh under cold water, then lay the leaves on a board and pat dry with paper towel. Cut either side of the stalk, discard the stalk and press the two halves of the leaf together, overlapping slightly so there are no gaps.

3 Lay 2 slices of pancetta on top of each cabbage leaf. Top with a heaped spoonful of the lamb mixture. Roll up tightly, folding in the ends to secure the filling. Insert a toothpick if necessary.

4 Arrange the cabbage rolls seam side down in a lightly greased baking dish. Pour over the stock, cover tightly with foil and bake for 10–15 minutes, or until cooked through. Arrange the rolls in serving bowls, spoon over some of the stock, season with salt and pepper and serve.

Spiced crumbed pork with carrot salad

Serves 4

4 pork leg steaks or medallions
1 tablespoon coriander seeds
1 tablespoon yellow mustard seeds
1 teaspoon garlic granules
1 tablespoon sesame seeds
2 teaspoons sweet paprika
2 cups soft breadcrumbs
¼ cup plain flour
2 eggs, lightly whisked
olive oil, for cooking
lemon wedges, to serve

Carrot salad

¼ cup extra-virgin olive oil
1 orange, juiced
2 tablespoons currants
3 large carrots, peeled
1 green cucumber, peeled
¼ cup hazelnuts, roasted,
  roughly chopped

1 Place the pork between sheets of baking paper and pound with a meat mallet until nice and thin.

2 Place the coriander seeds, mustard seeds and garlic in a mortar and pound with a pestle until the coriander seeds are broken. Add the sesame seeds and paprika and pound until just combined. Transfer the blended spices to a shallow dish, add the breadcrumbs and stir to combine.

3 Place the flour and the egg in separate shallow bowls. Dip the pork into the flour, then the egg and then the breadcrumb mixture, pressing the breadcrumbs on firmly with fingertips. Place on a plate and refrigerate for 15 minutes if time permits.

4 For the carrot salad, combine the oil, 3 tablespoons of orange juice and salt and pepper in a large bowl and whisk to combine. Add the currants and stir to coat. Cover and set aside for 15 minutes. Coarsely shred the carrots and cucumber and set aside. Just before serving, add the carrot, cucumber and hazelnuts to the currants and toss to combine.

5 Preheat the oven to 150°C fan-forced. Heat the oil in a large non-stick frying pan over medium heat. Add 2 pieces of pork and cook for 3–4 minutes on each side, or until golden and just cooked through. Transfer to a wire rack and keep warm in the oven while cooking the remaining 2 pieces of pork. Serve the pork with the carrot salad.

Sticky pork skewers with citrus salad

Pork with citrus is a real favourite. Pork belly is almost as common as mince these days, available from the butcher or from supermarkets. For the best price, try Asian butcher shops.

Serves 4

1.5kg boneless pork belly,
  rind removed ♥

¼ cup soy sauce

¾ cup brown sugar

1 cup water

2 star-anise

1 teaspoon Chinese five-spice powder

4 French shallots, finely chopped

2 garlic cloves, crushed

1 tablespoon peanut oil

steamed jasmine rice, to serve

Citrus salad

4 oranges

2 tablespoons extra-virgin olive oil

1 teaspoon sesame oil

½ teaspoon caster sugar

1 continental cucumber, peeled

3 green onions, thinly sliced

♥ You can use pork rashers for this recipe, also known as boneless pork ribs.

1 Preheat the oven to 130°C fan-forced. Cut the pork into 3cm pieces, then thread onto skewers and place in a roasting pan in a single layer.

2 Combine the soy, sugar, water, star-anise, five-spice, shallots and garlic in a bowl, then pour over the pork. Turn to coat. Cover the pork skewers tightly with two layers of foil and cook for 3 hours. Transfer the pork to a tray and strain the sauce into a saucepan. Place the saucepan over medium-high heat and bring to the boil, then boil uncovered for 10–15 minutes, or until thick and syrupy.

3 Meanwhile, for the citrus salad, peel and segment the oranges. Place the orange segments in a bowl. Squeeze the leftover pith into a jug until you have 2 tablespoons of liquid. Add the extra-virgin olive oil, sesame oil, sugar and salt and pepper and whisk until well combined. Cut the cucumber in half lengthways and remove the seeds. Thinly slice the cucumber and add to the orange segments with the green onions. Pour over the dressing and toss gently to combine.

4 Preheat a barbecue plate on medium-high. Brush both sides of the skewers with oil and barbecue for 4–6 minutes on each side, basting generously with the cooked marinade until golden and sticky. Serve with rice and the citrus salad.

Meatballs with roasted tomato sauce

Everyone needs a fabulous go-to meatball recipe. Here's mine.

Serves 4

1kg ripe tomatoes, halved ★
¼ teaspoon caster sugar
1 brown onion, cut into wedges
3 garlic cloves, halved
6 thyme sprigs
2 fresh bay leaves
¼ cup extra-virgin olive oil
1 cup kalamata olives, optional
½ cup basil leaves

Meatballs

375g pork mince
375g veal or beef mince
1 cup soft breadcrumbs
1 brown onion, grated
1 lemon, rind finely grated
1 tablespoon tomato paste
1 garlic clove, crushed
1 egg, lightly whisked
¼ cup basil leaves, finely chopped

★ This sauce is great with regular tomatoes, Roma tomatoes or cherry tomatoes. Check out which ones are cheaper by the kilo and use those.

1 For the meatballs, combine all the ingredients in a large bowl and season with salt and pepper. Using clean hands, mix until well combined. Using wet hands, roll spoonfuls of the mince mixture into balls and place on a tray. Cover and refrigerate for 30 minutes, or until firm.

2 Meanwhile, preheat the oven to 180°C fan-forced. Arrange the tomatoes in a lightly greased roasting pan, cut side up, and sprinkle with the sugar. Scatter over the onion, garlic, thyme and bay leaves. Drizzle with 2 tablespoons of olive oil and season well with salt and pepper. Roast for 45–60 minutes, or until the tomatoes are soft and light golden around the edges. Set aside to cool slightly. Discard the thyme and bay leaves. Spoon the mixture into a food processor and, depending on how you like your sauce, pulse until well combined or smooth.

3 Heat the remaining oil in a large non-stick frying pan over medium heat. Add half the meatballs and cook for 5–6 minutes, gently shaking the pan, until golden all over. Remove to a plate and repeat with the remaining meatballs.

4 Pour the tomato sauce into the same warm frying pan and place over medium heat. Stir through the olives and half the basil leaves. Add the meatballs and cook, uncovered, for 10 minutes, or until the meatballs are cooked through. If the sauce starts to thicken too much, add a little water. Season with salt and pepper, scatter over the remaining basil leaves and serve.

My new favourite pasta bake

I do love my job! This recipe came about when I was trying to use up the meatballs left over from the dish you can see on the previous page. We waste too much food, so before dialling for take-out, check the fridge and see what you can muster up.

Serves 6

375g large shell-shaped pasta ♥

1½ cups tomato passata (see page 122)

¼ cup flat-leaf parsley, roughly chopped

½ quantity cooked meatballs with roasted tomato sauce (see page 154) ★

125g ricotta

125g marinated feta

125g mozzarella, thinly sliced

♥ Large pasta shapes like the shells used here are available from greengrocers or specialty food stores. Smaller shapes will still work.

★ The meatballs with sauce can be hot or cold when added in step 2. The cooking time is a little shorter when they are hot.

1 Bring a large saucepan of salted water to the boil over high heat. Add the pasta and cook for half the time recommended on the packet. (The pasta needs to be firm and hold its shape.) Drain carefully.

2 Preheat the oven to 180°C fan-forced. Spoon the tomato passata over the base of a large lightly greased baking dish and stir in the parsley. Poke the pasta shells into the passata. Break the meatballs up and scatter over and into the pasta shells and sauce, then spoon over any leftover roasted tomato sauce. Crumble over the ricotta and feta, then top with the mozzarella. Cover tightly with a sheet of baking paper, then foil, and bake for 15 minutes until hot.

3 Increase the oven to 220°C fan-forced, remove the foil and paper and bake uncovered for 8–10 minutes, or until light golden on top. Season with salt and pepper and serve.

Mum's mustard veal

. . . .

Though our family was five, there was generally an extra body or two at our dinner table. This was one of the recipes my mum made almost every week.

Serves 6

12 small pieces veal steak or
   6 veal cutlets
2 tablespoons French mustard
⅓ cup plain flour
butter & olive oil, for cooking
1 cup chicken stock or water
steamed green beans, to serve

Parsley butter potatoes

750g kipfler, desiree or coliban potatoes,
   peeled, cut into 2cm pieces
60g butter, chopped
1 tablespoon olive oil
¼ cup flat-leaf parsley, chopped

1 Spread the mustard evenly over both sides of each piece of veal, then coat the veal well in flour seasoned with salt and pepper. (Don't shake off the excess – it helps form the sauce later.)

2 Preheat the oven to 130°C fan-forced. Heat a large non-stick frying pan over medium-high heat. Add a little butter and oil and swirl until melted and sizzling. Cook the veal, 2 pieces at a time, for 30–40 seconds on each side, until light golden, then transfer to a lightly greased baking dish. Repeat until all the veal is cooked. Cover to keep warm.

3 Add the stock or water to the hot frying pan, reduce the heat to medium and stir to loosen the sediment off the base of the pan. Pour the sauce over the veal, cover tightly with foil and place in the oven to cook for 30–40 minutes, until the veal has absorbed most of the pan juices. Wash and dry the frying pan.

4 For the parsley butter potatoes, place the potatoes in a saucepan and cover with cold water. Add a pinch of salt and bring to the boil over high heat. Reduce the heat to medium and cook, partially covered, for 8 minutes, or until the potatoes are just tender when tested with a skewer. Drain and return to the hot pan and cover to keep warm.

5 Heat the frying pan over medium-high heat. Add the butter and oil to the pan and swirl until melted. Add the potatoes and turn to coat in butter mixture. Cook for 5–6 minutes, or until they start to colour. Sprinkle over the parsley, season with salt and pepper and serve with the veal and green beans.

Slow-cooked beef stroganoff

Casseroles are always best made one or two days ahead, as the flavour really does improve. Leftovers never need be just leftovers – turn them into pies (see the recipe overleaf).

Serves 6

2 tablespoons tomato paste

2 cups beef stock

400g can diced tomatoes

1.25kg casserole beef (such as chuck or
   blade), cut into 3cm pieces

2 fresh (or 1 dried) bay leaves

1 cinnamon stick

2 tablespoons olive oil

30g butter

250g button mushrooms, trimmed

1 brown onion, halved, thinly sliced

1 tablespoon plain flour

1 tablespoon sweet paprika

½ cup sour cream

chopped flat-leaf parsley &
   cooked pasta, to serve

1 Preheat the oven to 130°C fan-forced. Combine the tomato paste, stock and tomatoes in an ovenproof casserole dish. Whisk to dissolve the tomato paste. Add the beef, bay leaves and cinnamon stick and stir to combine. The beef should be covered with the stock mixture. Press a piece of baking paper right down onto the surface and cover with a tight-fitting lid or double layer of foil. Place in the oven and cook for 4 hours, or until the beef is so tender it almost falls apart. Remove from the oven. ♥

2 Heat a deep, large non-stick frying pan over high heat until hot. Add 1 tablespoon of oil and the butter and mushrooms. Cook for 5 minutes, until light golden. Transfer the mushrooms to a plate. Reduce the heat to medium and add the remaining oil and onion, then cook, stirring, for 5–7 minutes, until soft.

3 Sprinkle the flour and paprika over the onions and cook, stirring, for 2 minutes. Add 1 cup of the liquid from the casserole and stir until the sauce comes to the boil. Reduce the heat to low, add the beef, all the remaining liquid from the casserole, and the mushrooms to the pan. Remove the bay leaves and cinnamon and simmer, uncovered, for 8–10 minutes, until the sauce thickens to the consistency you like. Taste, then season with salt and pepper.

4 Remove from the heat, swirl through the sour cream, sprinkle with parsley and serve over pasta, mashed potato or crusty bread.

♥ You can make the stroganoff up to this stage 1–2 days ahead, cool, then refrigerate.

Stroganoff pies

When making the stroganoff on the previous page, make double – the cooking time is the same – then set half aside to cool without adding the sour cream. Spoon it into containers and freeze or refrigerate it for up to 5 days, then turn it into the best pies the family has ever eaten.

Makes 8

1 quantity slow-cooked beef stroganoff (see page 161)
4 sheets ready rolled shortcrust pastry
4 sheets puff pastry (see notes, page ix)
1 egg, lightly beaten

1 Place a large flat baking tray in the oven. Preheat the tray and oven to 240°C fan-forced. Grease 8 × 9½cm (base) 1-cup capacity pie tins.

2 Cut two 14cm rounds from each shortcrust pastry sheet. Use to line the base and sides of the pie tins. Spoon the room-temperature beef stroganoff mixture into pastry. ★ Brush the pastry edges with cold water. Cut two 13cm rounds from each puff pastry sheet. Use to cover the filling, pressing the pastry edges together to seal. Trim any excess pastry, then brush the tops of the pies with egg and sprinkle with salt and pepper. Cut a small cross on top of each pie to allow excess steam to escape.

3 Place the pies on the hot baking tray. Reduce the oven to 220°C fan-forced and bake the pies for 25–30 minutes, or until the pastry is puffed and golden. Serve.

★ If the filling is warm the pastry will become soggy; if it is cold from the fridge it may not warm through by the time the pastry is golden and crisp.

Time for treats

Though I cook for a living, I bake for pleasure — and the sheer delight I get from serving treats to the people I love. It's something that runs in my family, so in this chapter I share a few more of my family recipes. As you remove my nan's Gugelhoph from the oven, as you dredge my mum's powder puffs with icing sugar, I hope you're as proud as they would be. Remember to hide away a little something sweet to treat yourself as well!

Raspberryoska

One of my most memorable meals started with the best cocktail I have ever consumed – a traditional caipiroska. The meal got better as each course was served. The restaurant was Longrain, the chef, Martin Boetz. This recipe is a variation of the original. For a less potent cocktail, fill your glass three-quarters full with raspberryoska, then top it up with lightly sparkling mineral water.

Makes 6–8

1 cup frozen raspberries
4 limes, chopped
1 tablespoon caster sugar
½ cup palm sugar syrup
1 cup crushed ice
250ml chilled vodka
chilled lightly sparkling mineral water,
  optional, to serve

Palm sugar syrup
1 cup chopped palm sugar ★
1 cup water

★ If you don't have palm sugar, you can replace it with raw sugar.

1 For the palm sugar syrup, combine the palm sugar and water in a saucepan over medium heat. Cook, stirring, for 5 minutes, until the sugar dissolves. Bring to the boil. Boil gently for 5–7 minutes, until the syrup reduces slightly. Set aside to cool. Pour into a sterilised jar. Refrigerate until cold.

2 Place the frozen raspberries, three-quarters of the limes and the sugar in a 2-litre (8-cup) heavy-duty glass jug. Use the end of a rolling pin to crush the berries, lime and sugar together. Stir in the chilled palm sugar syrup.

3 Add crushed ice so the jug is half full. Pour in the vodka and stir well. Pour into glasses. Add the remaining lime and serve immediately.

Lychee caipiroska – replace the raspberries with 1 cup of chilled canned lychees.

Pomegranate caipiroska – reduce the raspberries to ½ cup and add ¾ cup pomegranate juice.

Make-ahead breakfast fruit loaf

This fruit loaf freezes really well whole or in individual slices. It is delicious toasted under a grill or between sheets of baking paper in a sandwich press. Although I call it a breakfast loaf, it's scrumptious in a lunch box or any time of the day. You can use any combination of dried fruits, provided you include the 200 grams of dates.

Makes 12 slices

200g dried pitted dates, chopped
200g dried figs, chopped
100g dried apricots, chopped
100g raisins
2 cups water
1 teaspoon bicarbonate of soda
1 teaspoon ground cinnamon
1 teaspoon ground nutmeg
2 cups self-raising flour
¼ cup bran, optional
½ cup caster sugar
¼ cup extra-light olive oil
2 eggs
2 tablespoons mixed seeds

1 Preheat the oven to 180°C no fan/170°C fan-forced. Grease and line a 7cm-deep, 11cm × 21cm (base) loaf pan with baking paper.

2 Place the dates, figs, apricots, raisins and water in a medium saucepan over medium-high heat. Bring to the boil and then boil, uncovered, stirring occasionally, for 4 minutes. Approximately half the water should be absorbed by the fruit. Remove from the heat, cool for 5 minutes, then stir in the bicarbonate of soda. Once the bubbles have subsided a little, stir in the cinnamon and nutmeg. Set aside to cool for 20 minutes.

3 Sift the flour into a large bowl and stir in the bran, if using, and the caster sugar. Beat the oil and eggs together in a jug, then stir into the fruit. Spoon the fruit mixture into the flour and then stir until just combined.

4 Spread the mixture into the loaf pan and smooth the surface. Sprinkle the seeds over the top, pressing gently with your fingertips to secure them. Bake for 50–55 minutes, or until cooked through, when a skewer inserted into the centre comes out clean. If the top starts to brown too much, cover loosely with foil after 45 minutes. Cool completely in the pan.

5 Slice and serve with butter.

My nanna's chocolate Gugelhoph

I am convinced my love of chocolate and all things good came from my nan. She used to make this Gugelhoph for family brunch. She would feel the cake, hot out of the oven, to find the most chocolatey part, and cut that bit for me. She was and is a shining light in my heart.

Serves 8

1 cup milk

½ cup warm water

2 × 7g sachets instant dry yeast

pinch salt

1 teaspoon caster sugar

4 cups plain flour

1 teaspoon ground cinnamon

¼ cup brown sugar

60g butter, melted

1 egg, lightly beaten

400g good-quality dark chocolate, melted

1 cup walnuts, roughly chopped

icing sugar, to serve

1 Combine the milk and water in a saucepan over medium heat. Heat for 1–2 minutes, until lukewarm. Pour into a bowl, add the yeast, salt and sugar, then whisk to dissolve the yeast. Cover and set aside for 10 minutes.

2 Sift the flour and cinnamon together into a large bowl. Stir in the brown sugar. Add the butter, the egg and the yeast mixture and stir to form a soft dough. Turn onto a lightly floured surface and knead for 10 minutes, until the dough bounces back, leaving no indentation when touched with a fingertip. Place in a lightly greased bowl, cover with plastic wrap and a clean tea towel, then set aside for 30 minutes in a warm place, or until doubled in size.

3 Punch the dough down and knead it on a lightly floured surface for 5 minutes, until smooth and elastic. Roll the dough out to a 30cm × 40cm rectangle with the long side facing you. Spread the chocolate over the dough, then sprinkle the walnuts over the top. Roll it up like a Swiss roll, starting from the long side. Ease into a lightly greased 8-cup capacity Gugelhoph pan.★ Cover with plastic wrap and a tea towel and set aside in a warm place for 15–20 minutes, until doubled in size.

4 Preheat the oven to 200°C no fan/180°C fan-forced. Bake the Gugelhoph for 25–30 minutes, or until golden and cooked through. Stand for 5 minutes in the pan, then turn onto a board, dust with icing sugar and serve warm.

★ If you don't have a Gugelhoph pan, use a 23cm (base) springform pan. Grease the outside of an ovenproof glass or ramekin, pour in ¼ cup of water and place it in the centre of the pan to form the hole.

Melting moments

These biscuits remind me of my aunty Faye. No one bakes like she did – every biscuit perfect. The original CWA book calls them radio biscuits, but they are also known as custard kisses and yoyos.

Makes 32 single biscuits
250g butter, cubed
½ cup pure icing sugar, sifted
1 teaspoon vanilla essence
1¾ cups plain flour
⅓ cup custard powder

Passionfruit icing
2 cups pure icing sugar, sifted
1 tablespoon butter, softened
2 tablespoons fresh passionfruit pulp

1 Preheat the oven to 160°C fan-forced. Line two baking trays with baking paper.

2 Using an electric mixer, beat the butter, icing sugar and vanilla until pale and creamy. Sift the flour and custard powder together over the butter mixture and beat on low speed until the dough comes together. Refrigerate if the dough is soft.

3 Roll spoonfuls of the mixture into small balls. Place on a baking tray, leaving a little room for spreading. Dip a fork in a little flour, then use it to flatten each ball to about 3cm. Bake for 15–20 minutes, or until cooked through. Cool for 15 minutes on the trays, then transfer to a wire rack to cool. Repeat using the remaining mixture.

4 For the passionfruit icing, combine the icing sugar and butter in a bowl with just enough passionfruit pulp to form a thick icing.

5 Spread some passionfruit icing onto one biscuit and sandwich it together with another. Alternatively, warm the icing in a microwave for 30 seconds on High/100% and drizzle it over the biscuit tops. The biscuits are best filled or iced just before serving.

Caramel peanut butter kisses – whisk a 395g can of Top'n'Fill Caramel with ¼ cup peanut butter until smooth. Sandwich the biscuits together with the caramel filling.

Chocolate kisses – melt 200g dark chocolate with 2 tablespoons brewed espresso, stir until smooth, and refrigerate until the mixture is firm enough to spread. Sandwich the biscuits together with the chocolate filling.

Cut-out biscuits – at the end of step 2, roll the dough out between two sheets of baking paper until it is 5mm thin, then refrigerate until firm. Cut out shapes and refrigerate again until firm (this helps the biscuits hold their shape). Bake for 12 minutes. Dust with icing sugar or sandwich together with caramel or chocolate filling.

Raspberry & almond crumble slice

I tasted a slice like this when out one night, and was determined to recreate it. It took me weeks to get it right – balancing the crisp pastry with the tart berries and the golden crumble top. After testing it many times I finally perfected the recipe – it was all about the berries. You can use frozen berries, but only if you are going to bake and serve the slice within three hours. Frozen berries cause the crumble top to soften if it's left any longer.

Makes 16

1½ cups plain flour
¾ cup ground almonds
¾ cup caster sugar
200g butter, chopped
300g fresh raspberries, strawberries
  or blueberries
⅓ cup flaked almonds
icing sugar, to serve

1 Preheat the oven to 180°C fan-forced. Grease a 2½ cm-deep, 11cm × 34cm (base) rectangle flan pan. ★

2 Combine the flour, ground almonds, caster sugar and butter in a food processor. Process until the dough almost comes together. Transfer to a lightly floured bench and gently knead until smooth. Press two-thirds of the dough over the base of the prepared pan. Bake for 15–18 minutes, until light golden. Set aside to cool for 15 minutes.

3 Increase the oven to 200°C fan-forced. Scatter the raspberries over the lukewarm base. Crumble the remaining one-third of the dough evenly over the raspberries, then sprinkle with the almonds. Press down gently on the almonds and topping to secure them to the berries.

4 Bake for 25–30 minutes, or until the top is light golden. Allow to cool for 1 hour in the pan. Cut into fingers and serve lukewarm or at room temperature, dusted with icing sugar.

★ If you don't own a flat rectangular pan you can use a 20cm (base) square cake pan – just line the base and sides with baking paper so it's easy to lift the slice out when it is ready.

Mum's powder puffs

My sisters and I used to beg my mum to make these for us – she used to hide them from us in the downstairs fridge but we always found them. They're so light to eat, it's impossible to stop.

Makes 40

3 eggs, at room temperature
¾ cup caster sugar
½ cup plain flour
½ cup cornflour
2 teaspoons baking powder
450ml thickened cream
1 teaspoon vanilla extract
⅓ cup pure icing sugar ♥

♥ A delicious variation is to fold ½ cup of lemon or passionfruit curd through the whipped cream instead of the icing sugar.

1 Position the oven shelf in the centre of the oven and preheat the oven to 200°C fan-forced. Line 3 large flat trays with baking paper.

2 Using an electric mixer, beat the eggs and sugar on high speed for 8 minutes, or until the mixture is pale and thick, with the consistency of thickened cream. Sift the flours and baking powder together three times, and then a fourth time over the egg mixture. Gently fold together until just combined.

3 Drop 1 teaspoon of mixture onto a baking tray to form a small round and then repeat 6–8 times, allowing plenty of room for spreading. Bake, one tray at a time, for 4–6 minutes, or until light golden and firm to touch. Allow to cool on the tray for 10 minutes, until firm, then remove to a wire rack to cool completely. Repeat using the remaining mixture. (Don't worry – the mixture will become thicker while waiting to be baked.)

4 Whip the cream until thick. Stir in the vanilla and 2 tablespoons of the icing sugar, and whip until thick again. Sandwich the sponge rounds together with a dollop of whipped cream. Place in an airtight container, lining each layer with baking paper before placing the next layer on top. Refrigerate for 8–24 hours, or until soft to touch. Dust generously with the remaining icing sugar before serving.

Pistachio & chocolate tray tarts

I love exploring food markets (what a surprise!). On one of my recent trips to Melbourne I came across a whole range of gorgeous filo tarts filled with chocolate, nuts, dried fruit and so on – all attached to one another in trays. They became my inspiration for this recipe.

Makes 18

200g (1¼ cups) unsalted peanuts, roasted

200g (1 ⅓ cups) pistachio kernels, roasted

pinch salt

200g good-quality dark chocolate, melted

2 tablespoons honey

15 sheets filo pastry

125g clarified butter (ghee), melted

icing sugar, to serve

1 Pound the peanuts and pistachios with salt in a mortar with a pestle until finely crushed, or pulse them in a food processor. Transfer to a bowl, add melted chocolate and honey and mix until well combined.

2 Preheat the oven to 200°C fan-forced. Line a baking tray with baking paper.

3 Place the pastry sheets on a clean benchtop. Cover with a dry tea towel, then a damp tea towel (this will prevent it drying out). Brush 1 filo sheet with clarified butter, then top it with a second sheet. Repeat the process so you have five sheets layered on top of each other.

4 Place the pastry over the top of a 6-hole flat-based patty pan tray. Carefully press the pastry into the holes so the tray and holes are covered with filo. Spoon the pistachio mixture into each pastry hole to fill it. Bake for 12–15 minutes, or until the pastry is golden and crisp. Allow to cool in the pan. Carefully turn out onto the tray lined with baking paper, then invert back onto a wire rack, leaving all the tarts attached to each other. Repeat twice to use the remaining pastry and filling.

5 To serve, break or cut the tarts apart. Dust with icing sugar and serve.

Sour cream cake with drizzly lemon icing

I first enjoyed this moist, light cake while sipping a cold glass of bubbles (or it may have been a G & T) at my dearest friend Robyn's. One of her friends, Lisa, had made it and was happy to share it with us all. I have tweaked the cake and added the drizzly icing. It's gorgeous – enjoy sharing it with your friends!

Serves 8

125g butter, softened

2 lemons, rind finely grated, juiced

1 cup caster sugar

3 eggs, at room temperature

1 cup plain flour

½ teaspoon baking powder

⅓ cup sour cream

½ cup white sugar

1 Preheat the oven to 180°C no fan/170°C fan-forced. Grease and line the base and sides of a 5½cm-deep, 9cm ×19cm (base) loaf pan.

2 Using an electric mixer, beat the butter, lemon rind and caster sugar until pale and creamy. Add the eggs one at a time, beating well between additions (the mixture may look a little curdled). Sift the flour and baking powder together over the butter mixture and stir gently until combined.

3 Fold in the sour cream. Spread the mixture into the prepared pan and bake for 50–60 minutes, until a skewer inserted into the centre comes out clean. Stand in the pan for 10 minutes before turning onto a wire rack.

4 Combine the white sugar and ¼ cup of the lemon juice in a bowl, then quickly spoon the mixture over the warm loaf. Set aside to crystallise and cool.

Naomi's nougat

. . . .

My dear friend Naomi is an amazing cook and this is one of her specialties. We recently had a cooking (and eating)
day/night and she finally taught me how to make her nougat, so I could share it with you.

Makes about 60 pieces

500g almonds, skin on
250g pistachio kernels
4 sheets edible rice paper
1½ cups caster sugar
1 cup liquid glucose
½ cup water
¼ cup honey
2 × 65g eggs, separated ♥
pinch cream of tartar
170g dried cranberries

♥ I recommend using large 65g
eggs here, rather than the standard
59g eggs. This recipe only calls for
the whites – use the leftover yolks to
make coconut custard (see page 97).

1 Preheat the oven to 130°C fan-forced. Place the almonds and
pistachio kernels on a baking tray lined with baking paper and roast
them for 25–30 minutes.

2 Line the base of a 3cm-deep, 20cm × 30cm baking tray with baking
paper. Cut two sheets of rice paper to fit the base and place them on
top of the baking paper.

3 Combine the sugar, glucose, water and honey in a saucepan and stir
over a low heat until the sugar has dissolved. Brush down the sides
of the pan using a wet pastry brush. Increase to a medium heat and,
using a candy thermometer, cook the syrup, without stirring, to a
temperature of 140°C.

4 Meanwhile, once the syrup reaches 135°C, use an electric mixer ★
to beat the egg whites and cream of tartar to soft peaks. Turn the
mixer to low speed, slowly drizzle the hot syrup onto the egg whites
and continue to beat, pouring the syrup in a slow, steady stream. Once
all the syrup has been added, beat for a further 3 minutes on low
speed. The nougat will eventually start to thicken, so be patient.

5 Fold in the cranberries and warm nuts. Spoon the nougat into the
prepared pan and flatten it with a wet metal spoon. Cover with the
remaining sheets of rice paper, trimming to fit. Refrigerate overnight
until firm. Cut into pieces to serve.

★ You need an electric mixer with a heat-proof bowl for this recipe. A hand mixer will burn out.

Chocolate cherry cheesecake

This is decadent, delicious and one of my favourite food combinations.

Serves 12

500g cream cheese, chopped

1 cup caster sugar

2 eggs

300ml sour cream

1 cup drained, pitted Morello cherries ♥

icing sugar, to serve

Chocolate base

200g good-quality dark chocolate,
    chopped

200g butter, chopped

¼ cup cocoa powder

1 cup caster sugar

2 eggs

½ cup plain flour, sifted

¼ cup self-raising flour, sifted

¼ cup ground almonds

♥ When fresh cherries are
in season, use 375 grams.
Remember to remove the pips!

1 Preheat the oven to 180°C no fan/160°C fan-forced. Grease and line a 5cm-deep, 21cm × 30cm (base) slab pan.

2 For the chocolate base, combine the chocolate and butter in a microwave-safe heat-proof bowl. Microwave, uncovered, for 2 minutes on High/100%, stirring with a metal spoon until smooth. Add the cocoa powder to the warm chocolate mixture and whisk until dissolved. Stir in the caster sugar and eggs followed by the flours and ground almonds. Spread the mixture over the base of the pan and bake for 15 minutes (the base will still be soft). Remove from the oven and set aside for 20 minutes to firm up.

3 Preheat the oven to 160°C no fan/150°C fan-forced. Combine the cream cheese and caster sugar in a food processor and process until smooth. Add the eggs and sour cream and pulse until just combined. Carefully pour the cheesecake mixture over the warm chocolate base. Press the cherries into the cheesecake mixture and bake for 55–60 minutes or until the centre is firm.

4 Turn the oven off and leave the door ajar for 3 hours, then refrigerate the cheesecake overnight. Dust with icing sugar, cut into pieces and serve.

Chocolate rhubarb waffle pudding

This pudding is the perfect indulgent winter dessert.

Serves 8

1 bunch rhubarb, trimmed, chopped, washed ★
½ cup raw sugar
300g frozen waffles, lightly toasted
4 eggs
1 teaspoon vanilla extract
600ml thickened cream
200g good-quality milk or white chocolate, roughly chopped
icing sugar, to serve

★ If you like, replace the rhubarb with 1 cup frozen raspberries or blueberries. Ignore step 2 of the recipe and just scatter the frozen berries over in step 4.

1 Lightly grease 8 × 1-cup capacity ovenproof cups or 1 × 8-cup capacity ovenproof dish.

2 Toss the rhubarb in 1 tablespoon of the sugar and place on a microwave-safe plate. Cover and microwave for 2 minutes on High/100%, until warm (the rhubarb should still hold its shape). Set aside to cool for 15 minutes.

3 Cut the waffles into 3cm cubes. Using an electric hand mixer, beat the eggs, vanilla and remaining sugar in a large bowl until pale and thick. Add the cream and beat on low speed until just combined.

4 Arrange one-third of the waffles over the base of the cups or dish. Pour over one-third of the cream mixture. Top with one-third of the chocolate and one-third of the rhubarb. Repeat the layers twice. Allow to stand for 30 minutes (this allows the waffles to absorb the custard, producing a lighter pudding). Preheat the oven to 160°C fan-forced.

5 Place on a baking tray and bake, uncovered, for 40–50 minutes ♥ or until the custard is set and the top is golden. Dust with icing sugar and serve.

♥ Check the pudding after 40 minutes. If the tops are becoming too dark, cover them loosely with foil. This will depend on the waffles you use.

Torta della nonna

Torta della nonna *means grandmother's cake. It's the Tuscan version of a custard tart. The three best custard tarts in the world (in my opinion, and I have tasted many) are Portuguese, Greek and* torta della nonna.

Serves 8
4 egg yolks
¾ cup caster sugar
1 teaspoon vanilla bean paste
⅓ cup plain flour
2½ cups milk
250g ricotta
2 tablespoons pine nuts
icing sugar, to serve

Pastry
2 cups plain flour
⅓ cup caster sugar
150g butter, chilled, chopped
1-2 tablespoons iced water

♥ Feel the pastry – if it is still nice and firm and cool to touch, sprinkle a little flour over the surface and proceed. If not, refrigerate it for a further 10 minutes until it feels cool.

1 Whisk the egg yolks, ½ cup of the sugar and the vanilla in a large bowl until pale. Add the flour and beat until well combined. Add ¼ cup milk and whisk until smooth, then pour in the remaining milk, whisking constantly to prevent lumps. Pour the egg mixture into a medium saucepan and cook over medium-high heat, stirring constantly, until the custard just comes to the boil. Pour into a clean bowl, cover the surface with plastic wrap and refrigerate overnight.

2 For the pastry, combine the flour, sugar and butter in a food processor. Process until the mixture resembles fine breadcrumbs. Add 1 tablespoon of the water and process until the pastry just comes together in a ball, adding the remaining water if necessary. Turn onto a lightly floured surface and knead gently until smooth.

3 Remove one-third of the pastry and press it into a 10cm round. Wrap it in greaseproof paper (don't use plastic, as this causes the pastry to sweat) and refrigerate for 15 minutes, or until firm enough to roll out. Place the remaining two-thirds of the pastry between two large sheets of baking paper. Roll the pastry out to a 30cm disc. Remove the top sheet of baking paper ♥ and lift the pastry into a lightly greased 22cm (base) flan tin. The pastry should sit 1cm above the top of the tin. Refrigerate for 10 minutes.

4 Using a hand mixer, beat the ricotta and the remaining ¼ cup of caster sugar until well combined. Add the chilled custard and beat until just combined. Spoon the custard into the pastry. Carefully fold the excess pastry over the custard and brush with water. Roll the remaining pastry out until it is 5mm thick, then cut a 20cm round from the pastry. Sprinkle the pine nuts over it, then gently roll them into the pastry. Place the pastry over the tart and press to secure. Refrigerate for 10 minutes while the oven preheats.

5 Preheat the oven and a large flat baking tray to 200°C fan-forced. Place the tart on the hot tray and bake for 15 minutes, then reduce the oven to 180°C fan-forced and bake for a further 35–40 minutes, or until golden. Set aside to cool to room temperature. Dust heavily with icing sugar and serve.

Baked chocolate hazelnut mousse cake with espresso cream

Serves 8

melted butter & white sugar, for coating

250g butter, chopped

400g good-quality dark chocolate

¼ cup cocoa powder

1 cup hazelnuts, roasted ★

5 eggs

¾ cup caster sugar

¼ cup self-raising flour, sifted

cocoa powder, to serve

Espresso cream

2 tablespoons instant espresso
  coffee powder

2 teaspoons warm water

300ml double cream

★ I like to roast my own hazelnuts and then grind them – the flavour is better, and it's cheaper.

1 Preheat the oven to 180°C no fan. Turn the base of an 8cm-deep, 22cm (base) springform pan upside down, so the flat side faces up. Top with a sheet of baking paper, then lock into position. Grease the base and side with melted butter, then sprinkle with white sugar to coat (this gives the cake a crust and helps it rise).

2 Place the butter and chocolate in a microwave-safe, heat-proof bowl. Microwave uncovered for 2–3 minutes on High/100%, stirring every minute with a metal spoon until it is melted and smooth. Add the cocoa powder to the warm mixture and whisk until smooth. Set aside for 10 minutes.

3 Place the hazelnuts in a food processor and process until very fine. Using an electric mixer, beat the eggs and caster sugar together for 6–8 minutes on high speed until thick and pale. Add the chocolate mixture, hazelnuts and flour and stir to combine.

4 Pour the mixture into the cake pan. Place on a tray and bake for 20 minutes, then cover the top loosely with a piece of foil and bake for a further 40 minutes, until a skewer inserted into the centre has moist crumbs clinging to it. Set aside to cool completely in the pan.

5 For the espresso cream, dissolve the coffee powder in the water in a medium bowl. Cool for 5 minutes. Add the cream and stir gently with a balloon whisk until combined and thick enough to dollop.

6 Dust the cake heavily with cocoa powder, cut into wedges with a warm knife and serve with espresso cream.

Roasted plums with ricotta fritters

Makes 6

12 plums, halved, stones removed

2 tablespoons white sugar

Ricotta fritters

1 cup ricotta ★

¼ cup caster sugar

⅓ cup self-raising flour

1 egg yolk

1 teaspoon vanilla extract

2 tablespoons white sugar

2 teaspoons ground cinnamon

vegetable oil, for deep-frying

★ If time permits, place the ricotta in a sieve, cover it, and refrigerate overnight to drain the excess liquid. The fritters will be firmer in texture.

1 Preheat the oven to 230°C fan-forced. Line a roasting pan with baking paper. Place the plums cut side up in the pan. Sprinkle the sugar over the cut side of the plums. Roast for 5–7 minutes, until the sugar has dissolved but the plums still hold their shape. Remove from the oven and set aside to cool slightly.

2 For the ricotta fritters, crumble the ricotta into a large bowl. Add the caster sugar, flour, egg yolk and vanilla and beat with a wooden spoon until well combined.

3 Combine the white sugar and cinnamon together on a plate. Half-fill a saucepan with oil and heat it over medium heat until hot.

4 Drop small spoonfuls of the ricotta mixture into the oil and deep-fry for 3–4 minutes, turning occasionally until golden. Use a slotted spoon to remove the fritters from the oil and toss quickly but gently in the cinnamon sugar. Repeat using the remaining fritter mixture. Serve the hot fritters with the plums.

Tiramisu ice-cream with chocolate-coated cones

Simply irresistible!

Serves 10

200g good-quality dark chocolate,
    chopped
⅓ cup thickened cream
1.5 litres vanilla ice-cream
¼ cup strong brewed coffee
¼ cup coffee liqueur (such as Kahlúa)
12 sponge finger biscuits,
    roughly chopped

Chocolate-coated cones

200g good-quality dark chocolate,
    chopped
2 tablespoons thickened cream
10 waffle ice-cream cones

1 Combine the chocolate and cream in a heat-proof, microwave-safe bowl. Microwave, uncovered, on High/100% in 1 minute bursts, stirring every minute with a metal spoon until it is melted and smooth. Set aside to cool for 15 minutes.

2 Remove the ice-cream from the freezer and set aside for 10–20 minutes to soften slightly. Combine the coffee and liqueur in a jug.

3 Scatter one-third of the sponge finger biscuits over the base of a 2-litre capacity loaf dish or container. Spoon over one-third of the coffee mixture. Spoon one-third of the ice-cream over the biscuits, then spoon over one-third of the chocolate sauce. Repeat the layers twice, finishing with the chocolate sauce. Cover and freeze overnight.

4 For the chocolate-coated cones, combine the chocolate and cream in a heat-proof, microwave-safe bowl. Microwave, uncovered, on High/100% in 1 minute bursts, stirring every minute with a metal spoon until it is melted and smooth. Set aside to cool for 10 minutes. Spoon a heaped tablespoon of chocolate mixture into each ice-cream cone and swirl to coat the inside, then turn upside down on a piece of baking paper and allow to set.

5 Scoop the ice-cream into the cones and serve immediately.

Profiteroles with tiramisu ice-cream & hot fudge sauce

One of my dreams when I was a student was to open a profiterole shop. I used to make them by the hundreds and sell them to pay my way while studying. They are still the number one request from my dearest friends. They look fancy but they're the easiest pastry to master – just follow the recipe.

Makes 12

125g butter, chopped
1 cup lukewarm water
1 cup plain flour
4 × 55g eggs, lightly beaten
1 quantity tiramisu ice-cream
  (see previous page)

Hot fudge sauce
¼ cup strong brewed espresso coffee
¼ cup thickened cream
200g good-quality dark chocolate

1 Place one shelf just above the centre and one shelf just below the centre position in the oven and preheat to 220°C fan-forced. Line 2 baking trays with baking paper.

2 Melt the butter in a medium saucepan over medium heat and, as soon as it is melted, add the water. Increase the heat to high and bring to a rolling boil (the liquid should start to rise in the pan).

3 Remove from the heat and quickly add all the flour at once, stirring constantly with a wooden spoon until the mixture comes together in a ball and comes away from the sides of the saucepan. Transfer the hot dough to the bowl of an electric mixer. Beating on medium speed, add a quarter of the egg and beat until well combined. Continue adding the egg until the mixture is thick and shiny. ♥

4 Spoon or pipe the choux pastry onto the trays, allowing room for spreading. Bake for 10 minutes. Reduce the oven to 200°C fan-forced and bake for a further 15–20 minutes, or until the choux pastry is puffed, golden and firm to touch. (The lower tray may require longer; if so, quickly remove the top tray and reposition the second tray on the top shelf). Allow to cool completely on the trays.

5 For the hot fudge sauce, combine the coffee, cream and chocolate in a heat-proof, microwave-safe jug or bowl. Microwave, uncovered, for 2–3 minutes on High/100%, stirring every minute with a metal spoon until melted and smooth, adding more brewed coffee to adjust the consistency if required.

6 Cut the profiteroles in half with kitchen scissors. Fill with tiramisu ice-cream and place on serving plates. Pour over the hot fudge sauce and serve.

♥ This is a crucial stage. The pastry needs to be thick and shiny, not runny. It may not take all the egg – at times you may find that you have 1–2 tablespoons of egg left over.

Deep-fried ice-cream

Just saying deep-fried ice-cream out loud might make you feel guilty – not I! When it's homemade, this special treat is as good as anything I have tasted. This recipe is a slight variation on an original created by a beautiful gentle soul I used to work with – Kerrie Mullins.

Serves 4

1 litre vanilla ice-cream
450g packet Madeira cake
   (Top Taste brand)
2 eggs
1 cup dried breadcrumbs
vegetable oil, for deep-frying
real caramel sauce, to serve
   (see page 93)
icing sugar, to serve

1 Scoop 4 large scoops of ice-cream onto a tray lined with baking paper and freeze for 3–4 hours, or until firm.

2 Cut 8 × 1cm-thick slices from the cake. Place a slice of cake in the palm of your hand and top it with a scoop of ice-cream. Place a second piece of cake over the ice-cream and use your hands to mould the cake around the ice-cream, ensuring the ice-cream is completely covered. Place on a tray and return to the freezer. Repeat with the remaining cake and ice-cream and freeze the balls for 3–6 hours, until firm.

3 Beat the eggs in a shallow bowl and place the breadcrumbs in a shallow dish. Take one ice-cream ball at a time and roll it in the egg, then coat in the breadcrumbs. Return to the freezer after coating. Repeat the egg and breadcrumb layers to form a double coating. Freeze for 3 hours or overnight. ★

4 Pour oil into a large heavy-based saucepan or wok until it is one-third full and heat it over medium heat until hot. Remove the ice-cream balls from the freezer and let stand for 5 minutes before cooking.

5 Drop 2 balls into the oil at a time and cook for 1 minute, or until golden. Drain on a wire rack, then serve immediately, drizzled with hot caramel sauce and dusted with icing sugar.

★ You can make the ice-cream balls and then stop at this step, keeping them in the freezer for up to 2 weeks.

Upside down berry pavlova

This is a great dessert everyone loves, and it looks impressive for very little effort. You can use frozen berries or fresh – shop around and see what's cheaper.

Serves 6–8

750g fresh strawberries
300g frozen pitted cherries
2 tablespoons white sugar
4 egg whites, at room temperature
pinch cream of tartar
¾ cup caster sugar
2 tablespoons cocoa powder

1 Preheat the oven to 220°C fan-forced. Lightly grease a 4cm-deep, 18cm × 25cm (base) baking dish.

2 Hull and halve the strawberries and place in the baking dish. Add the frozen cherries. Sprinkle over the white sugar and shake the dish gently to coat all the fruit. Place in the oven and roast for 5 minutes. Remove from the oven and set aside. Reduce the oven to 130°C fan-forced.

3 Using an electric mixer, beat the egg whites and cream of tartar until soft peaks form. Add the caster sugar one spoonful at a time, beating well between each spoonful until the meringue is thick and glossy. Sift over the cocoa powder and swirl through.

4 Drop large spoonfuls of meringue over the warm fruit. Bake for 30–40 minutes, or until the meringue is firm to touch. Turn the oven off, open the door slightly and allow to stand for 10 minutes before serving. Serve warm or at room temperature.

Mandarin & passionfruit jelly with little coconut meringues

Gelatine is an ingredient that scares many people. If that's you, this recipe will boost your confidence. It's foolproof – not to mention stunning! Packet jelly just doesn't compare.

Makes 6

4 teaspoons powdered gelatine

¾ cup cold water

½ cup caster sugar

1¾ cups freshly squeezed mandarin juice

½ cup fresh passionfruit pulp

Little coconut meringues ♥

1½ cups shredded or flaked coconut

2 egg whites, at room temperature

pinch cream of tartar

½ cup caster sugar

1 teaspoon vanilla extract

♥ This recipe makes 60 little coconut meringues. Leftovers are delicious sandwiched together with lemon curd (see page 79) or caramel peanut butter (see page 172).

1 Combine the gelatine and cold water in a small saucepan. Place over medium heat and stir for 4–5 minutes, until the liquid turns clear. Add the sugar and mandarin juice and heat for a further 3 minutes, stirring until the sugar has dissolved. Remove from the heat.

2 Strain the passionfruit pulp, discard the seeds and pour the juice into the mandarin mixture. Pour into a jug and refrigerate for 15–20 minutes, until cold, then pour into 6 × 1-cup capacity serving glasses. Cover and refrigerate 6 hours, until set.

3 For the little coconut meringues, preheat the oven to 150°C fan-forced. Line 2 baking trays with baking paper. Spread the coconut over 1 tray and cook for 3–4 minutes in the oven, or until lightly toasted. Transfer to a plate to cool. Using an electric mixer, beat the egg whites and cream of tartar until soft peaks form. Add the sugar a spoonful at a time, beating well between each spoonful. Fold in the vanilla and toasted coconut. Drop small spoonfuls of the mixture onto trays, allowing a little room for spreading. Bake for 20 minutes, or until firm to touch. Turn the oven off, open the door and allow the meringues to cool on the trays.

4 Just before serving, drop a few little coconut meringues on top of each jelly, drizzle with extra passionfruit pulp if desired, and serve.

Lime & coconut puddings with palm sugar syrup

These gorgeous golden coconut-scented mounds can be made ahead and even frozen. You can warm them from room-temperature in a 160°C fan-forced oven for 15 minutes or microwave them for 3–4 minutes on Medium/50%, covered loosely with a damp paper towel.

Makes 6

150g butter, softened

1 cup caster sugar

1 teaspoon vanilla extract

2 limes, rind finely grated

2 eggs

1½ cups self-raising flour, sifted

½ cup desiccated coconut

1 cup coconut milk

1½ cups warm palm sugar syrup
  (see page 82)

toasted shredded coconut
  & double cream, to serve

1 Preheat the oven to 170°C fan-forced. Lightly grease 6 × 1-cup capacity ovenproof ramekins or moulds. Line the base of each with a round of baking paper.

2 Using an electric mixer, beat the butter, sugar, vanilla and lime together until pale and creamy. Add the eggs one at a time, beating well after each addition. Fold in the flour and coconut, then the coconut milk, until just combined.

3 Spoon the mixture evenly among the ramekins, then place in a roasting pan. Pour enough boiling water into the pan to come halfway up the sides of the ramekins. Place a round of baking paper over the top of each pudding, then cover the roasting pan tightly with foil. Bake for 30–35 minutes, or until a skewer inserted into the centre of a pudding comes out clean.

4 Remove ramekins from the water bath and cover them loosely with a clean tea towel. Allow to stand for 10 minutes. Turn the puddings onto serving plates, pour over plenty of warm palm sugar syrup, top with toasted shredded coconut and serve with cream.

Incy wincy christmas puddings

These little puddings have been part of our family Christmas for many years. They are a great thing to end the meal on or to package up as gifts for family, friends or schoolteachers. They'll keep for 2–3 weeks in an airtight container lined with foil – add the fondant stars just before you want to eat them!

Makes about 60

200g pitted dates, chopped
200g dried figs, chopped
150g raisins, chopped
100g sultanas
200g glacé fruit, chopped
   (such as pineapple, apricot & cherries)
2 teaspoons ground nutmeg
1 teaspoon ground cinnamon
1 teaspoon ground ginger
¾ cup brandy or coffee liqueur
   (such as Kahlúa)
185g butter, softened
⅓ cup dark brown sugar
¼ cup golden syrup
3 eggs
⅓ cup plain flour, sifted
3 cups soft breadcrumbs
200g good-quality white chocolate,
   chopped
icing sugar or fondant shapes & cachous,
   to decorate

1 Combine the dates, figs, raisins, sultanas, glacé fruit and spices in a large heat-proof bowl. Warm the brandy or liqueur in a small saucepan over medium-high heat and then pour over the fruit mixture. Stir to combine, cover and set aside overnight.

2 Using an electric mixer, beat the butter, sugar and golden syrup until well combined. Add the eggs one at a time, beating well after each addition. Stir in the flour, then the breadcrumbs. Add the fruit mixture and chocolate and stir until well combined.

3 Preheat the oven to 150°C fan-forced. Lightly grease 2 × 12-hole mini muffin pans. Spoon the mixture into the muffin pans until full. Bake for 20–25 minutes, or until a skewer inserted into the centre of a pudding comes out clean. Allow to stand for 5 minutes in the pan before turning onto a wire rack to cool. Repeat twice to make remaining puddings.

4 To make the fondant shapes, tint ready-bought fondant with food colouring. Roll it out between 2 sheets of baking paper lightly dusted with icing sugar. Cut it into shapes and place on a tray lined with baking paper. Stand overnight to dry. Attach to puddings with a little melted chocolate.

Crème caramel

Visitors to my website and callers who ring in when I'm doing talkback radio are always asking me for a crème caramel recipe that works every time. My secret is a touch of cornflour – it guarantees success.

Makes 6

1 cup white sugar

300ml milk

450ml thickened cream

4 eggs, at room temperature

4 egg yolks

²/₃ cup caster sugar

1 teaspoon vanilla bean paste

1 teaspoon cornflour

1 Position the oven shelf in the centre of the oven and preheat to 160°C no fan. Line the base of a large roasting pan with a tea towel, folded to fit. Place 6 ungreased 200ml-capacity ovenproof ramekins into the pan on the tea towel. ♥

2 Pour the white sugar into a small non-stick frying pan and place over medium-high heat. Cook, stirring and tilting the pan occasionally, until the sugar dissolves and turns a deep caramel colour. Pour the caramel evenly into the base of the ramekins. Place in the lined roasting pan and set aside to cool.

3 Combine the milk and cream in a medium saucepan over medium heat. Warm for 5 minutes, but don't allow it to boil. Using a fork, whisk the eggs, egg yolks, caster sugar, vanilla and cornflour in a large heat-proof bowl until combined. Gradually add the warm milk mixture, stirring constantly to prevent the eggs cooking. Strain the mixture into a jug.

4 Pour the custard evenly over the toffee and cover each ramekin with a piece of foil. Pour enough hot water into the roasting pan to reach halfway up the side of the ramekins. Bake for 35–40 minutes, or until a metal skewer inserted in the centre of the custard comes out clean or with just a little softly set custard clinging to it.

5 Carefully remove the ramekins from the water bath and set aside for 2 hours. Remove the foil and cover each with plastic wrap, place on a tray and refrigerate for 24–48 hours. This allows the toffee to dissolve and produce caramel.

6 Carefully run a thin sharp knife around the side of the ramekins and turn the custards onto a serving plate with a lip. Serve.

♥ The tea towel protects the crème caramel from the excessive heat at the base of the water bath, preventing the custard from overcooking and curdling.

Time & food to share

Choosing recipes for a special event is no easy task. We all ask the same questions — Will there be enough food? How much preparation can I do? Am I going to be in the kitchen while everyone else is enjoying themselves? The menus in this section remove all the guesswork, so when next you plan an occasion, it's a memorable one for you and for your family and friends.

Christmas lunch or dinner

I love Christmas. It's about food, family gatherings and the gift of giving and sharing – all things that are very important to me. It's also one time of year that many of us cook for a bigger crowd than we're used to, so attention to detail is paramount! This menu gives a well-balanced spread with plenty of colour and flavour – and it won't keep the hosts in the kitchen.

Menu for 12

· · · · · · · · · · · · · · · · · · · ·

3 × Raspberryoska (page 167)
2 × Thai chicken, mango & coconut salad with wontons (page 130)

2 × Roast turkey breast with hasselback potatoes (page 135)
2 × Prawn & watermelon salad (page 30)
2 × Waldorf salad (page 9)

2 × Toffee fruit with cheesecake ice-cream (page 90)

1 × Incy wincy puddings (page 208)
1 × Naomi's nougat (page 182)

Get organised

1 week ahead

Make the palm sugar syrup for the raspberryoska.
Place the vodka in the freezer to chill.
Start making ice for the drinks if necessary.

Order the turkey from the butcher.

Make the cream cheese ice-cream and store in the back of the freezer.

Make the incy wincy puddings and fondant shapes and store in separate airtight containers at room temperature.

Make the nougat and store uncut in the baking tray in an airtight container in the fridge.

Up to 2 days ahead

Make the dressing for the prawn and watermelon salad, and refrigerate.

Roast the walnuts for the Waldorf salad, then cool and refrigerate.

The day before

Make 1 quantity of driver/kid-friendly raspberryoska (no vodka!), following the recipe to the end of step 2. Cover and refrigerate.

Make the dressing for the Thai chicken, mango and coconut salad. Cook and shred the chicken, then store in an airtight container in the fridge.

Complete steps 1 and 2 of the roast turkey recipe. Wrap in greaseproof paper and store in an airtight container in the fridge.

Peel the prawns for the salad, place in an airtight container, cover with damp paper towel and refrigerate. Cut the watermelon into pieces and refrigerate in an airtight container. Toast the walnuts and sesame seeds, cool and refrigerate.

Attach the fondant shapes to the puddings.

Up to 4 hours before guests arrive

Cook 36 wontons for the Thai chicken, mango and coconut salad up to 4 hours before guests are expected. Prepare all the ingredients in step 3 and store in separate plastic bags in the fridge up to 4 hours ahead.

Complete steps 3–5 of the roast turkey recipe. Remove the turkey from the pan and set aside to rest. Cover the potatoes with a clean tea towel.

Complete steps 2 and 3 of the Waldorf salad. Dice the celery and shred the lettuce, then store in separate airtight containers in the fridge

Just before serving

Complete steps 2 and 3 of the raspberryoska. Add crushed ice to the driver/kid-friendly version and top up with sparkling mineral water to serve.

Toss the salad, chicken and dressing together for the Thai chicken, mango and coconut salad and pile onto wontons to serve.

20 minutes before serving the main, return the hasselback potatoes to the hot oven and roast until golden and crisp and warmed through.

Toss the prawn and watermelon salad ingredients together and pour over the dressing just before serving.

Toss the Waldorf salad ingredients together.

Make the toffee fruit for dessert while others are clearing away the main meal. Remove the ice-cream from the freezer 10–15 minutes before serving.

Cut the nougat into pieces up to 1 hour before serving.

Sunday brunch

Brunch in my world is a relaxed and often impromptu gathering of
family and friends, and the food and setting should reflect this.
A casual spread needn't take too much effort – or much shopping –
but just a little planning and cooking ahead means you are able to sit
back and enjoy your friends, the food and the conversation.

Menu for 8

4 × Custard apple & berry smoothie (page 64)

2 × Quiche lorraine (page 118)
2 × Lemon & garlic roast chicken (page 16)

1 × Cheat's almond croissants (page 71)
1 × Raspberry & white chocolate muffins (page 68)

Freshly brewed coffee

Extras
Crusty bread
300g mixed baby salad leaves
1 × salad dressing (see page 30)

Get organised

The day before
Make the cornmeal pastry for the quiche, then chop the ham and green onions.
Store in separate containers in the fridge.

Complete steps 1 and 2 of the lemon and garlic roast chicken recipe. Refrigerate overnight.

Complete step 1 of the almond croissant recipe. Store the croissants at room temperature in an airtight container.

Make the salad dressing and refrigerate.

Up to 4 hours before guests arrive
Make the muffins.

Scoop the flesh from the custard apples into a bowl, and refrigerate.

Complete steps 2–4 for the quiche lorraine.

Microwave the potatoes for the roast chicken.

Complete step 2 of the almond croissant recipe. Cover the croissants with a tea towel and set aside.

As the guests arrive
Make batches of smoothies.

After the guests have arrived
Complete steps 4 and 5 of the roast chicken recipe, then toss the salad dressing and baby salad leaves together at the table and serve.

After clearing away the savoury dishes
Bake the almond croissants and put on a pot of coffee. When the croissants have 5 minutes left to go, place the muffins underneath them in the oven to warm through. Serve both warm from the oven with the freshly brewed coffee.

Afternoon tea with the girls

Any excuse for a girlie gossip gathering is a godsend. We usually wait
for a baby shower or a kitchen tea to put on a fabulous spread, but let's
face it – they don't come around often enough. So, next time the boys
go to the football (though I love going too), plan a girlie day in.
(PS – Tell the boys there will be plenty of leftovers.)

Menu for 12

· ·

Pink champagne with raspberries

2 × Pork larb salad (page 45)

1 × Melting moments (page 172)
1 × Mum's powder puffs (page 176)
1 × Mum's poppyseed cake (page 80)
1 × Lemon meringue tartlets (page 79)
1 × Rum, raisin and honeycomb no-bake slice (page 76)

Get organised

2 days before

Chill the champagne.

Complete step 1 of the pork larb recipe. Refrigerate the garlic mixture and lime juice mixture in separate airtight containers.

Make the rum and raisin honeycomb no-bake slice. Once set, wrap tightly in plastic and store in the fridge.

Make the lemon curd for the lemon meringue tartlets and store in clean jars in the fridge.

The day before

Wash, dry and separate the leaves for the pork larb, then wrap in paper towel and store in a plastic bag in the crisper.

Bake the melting moments, then allow to cool and store in an airtight container lined with foil top and bottom.

Bake the poppyseed cake. Once cooled, store in an airtight container at room temperature. Make the cream cheese frosting and store in airtight container in the fridge.

Shape the biscuits and bake the meringues for the tartlets. Store in separate airtight containers at room temperature.

Make the powder puffs, then store in single layers between two sheets of baking paper in airtight containers in the fridge.

Up to 4 hours before guests arrive

Complete steps 2 and 3 of the pork larb recipe. Set aside at room temperature.

Cut no-bake slice into pieces, then cover and refrigerate until ready to serve.

Put the champagne glasses in the fridge to chill.

Ice the poppyseed cake.

Make the passionfruit icing for the melting moments. As close to serving as possible, sandwich or top the melting moments with icing, so that the biscuits stay crisp.

Just before serving

Spoon the larb into the lettuce leaves to serve.

Dust the no-bake slice with cocoa powder.

Fill the tartlets with lemon curd and top with meringue.

Dust the powder puffs with icing sugar.

Add the raspberries to the chilled champagne glasses as your guests arrive, and top with champagne.

Barbecue on the deck

Is there anything better than sitting outdoors enjoying fresh air with family and friends and breathing in the intoxicating aromas of food sizzling away on the barbecue? I don't think so. When the weather's fine, it's time to get outside. Turn up the sunshine dial, relax and enjoy the feast you have created. Tell your friends to bring their appetites!

Menu for 8

· ·

1 × Blender lemonade (see page 67)

1½ × Cajun chicken – hold the minted peas & rice (see page 19)
2 × Apple & mint lamb (see page 36)
1 × Chilli, mint & lime seared salmon (see page 33)
2 × Papaya & cucumber salad (see page 33)
1 × Fold-over barbecue pizza (see page 122)
2 × Corn & avocado salad (see page 15)

1 × Pavlova parfait (see page 94)
1 × Choc honeycomb crisps (see page 86)

Get organised

2 days before

Make the blender lemonade and store in the fridge. Chill the sparkling mineral water.

Make the tomato passata for the pizza, and refrigerate. Char-grill the capsicum and eggplant and refrigerate together in an airtight container.

Make the choc honeycomb crisps and refrigerate in an airtight container.

The day before

Marinate the chicken and refrigerate.

Marinate the lamb and refrigerate.

Make the dressing for the corn & avocado salad and refrigerate.

Complete steps 1–3 of the pavlova parfait recipe. Store in an airtight container at room temperature. Prepare the mango and passionfruit and store in separate containers in the fridge.

Up to 4 hours before guests arrive

Thread the chicken onto skewers, place on a plate and refrigerate. Wrap the tortillas in foil.

Cut the salmon into pieces and thread onto skewers, then make the marinade and refrigerate both separately. Prepare the papaya salad and dressing and refrigerate both separately.

Cook the corn, then add to the dressing. Cover and set aside at room temperature.

Make the pizza dough. After it has been kneaded in step 2, wrap tightly in plastic and refrigerate.

Up to 1 hour before guests arrive

Remove the pizza dough from the fridge and unwrap, then allow to stand at room temperature for 30 minutes. Complete step 3 of the recipe, then place the uncooked pizzas on a tray lined with baking paper, cover and refrigerate.

Barbecue the lamb and apples, place on a serving platter, cover with foil and set aside at room temperature to be served with main meal.

Just before serving

Fill jugs with ice and pour in the lemonade and mineral water. Put the jugs on the table for everyone to help themselves.

Barbecue the Cajun chicken; a few minutes before the chicken skewers are ready, place the wrapped tortillas on the barbecue to warm through. Place on a platter together and let people help themselves.

Marinade the salmon and then barbecue it. Place on a platter, cover and set aside while cooking the pizzas.

Barbecue the pizzas, then serve.

Toss the papaya salad and dressing together at the table just before serving. Serve with the salmon.

Cut the avocado and add to the corn and dressing with the salad leaves.

Whip the cream and assemble the pavlova parfaits, dividing the mixture between 8 × ¾-cup capacity glasses. Serve a glass of parfait to each guest or arrange on a large platter of crushed ice and allow guests to help themselves.

Bring out the choc honeycomb crisps to nibble on after dessert.

Portable picnic

Buying a barbecue chicken, pre-made salads and bread rolls is not only expensive but so yesterday when it comes to the picnic hamper. You will be pleasantly surprised by this lovely menu – it's quick, easy and deliciously tasty. When you roll out your picnic rug and pull out this spread, you and your family will be the envy of everyone else around, guaranteed!

Menu for 8

· ·

2 × Buttermilk chicken (page 129)
1 × Cheese & basil pull-apart (page 112)
2 × Carrot salad (page 150)

1 × Lemon blueberry friands (page 89)
1 × Happy face biscuits (page 72)

4 × Hot chocolate mallow sticks (page 72)

Biscuits

Get organised

The day before

Marinade the chicken in buttermilk and refrigerate. Combine seasoning in a bag and set aside at room temperature.

Make the dressing for the carrot salad, pour into a jar and refrigerate. Peel and shred the carrots and refrigerate in an airtight container. Roast the hazelnuts and store in an airtight container at room temperature.

Make the friands and store in an airtight container at room temperature.

Make the happy face biscuits and store in an airtight container.

Dip the marshmallows in chocolate and allow to set, then thread onto skewers, wrap in foil and refrigerate.

Up to 4 hours before leaving for the picnic

Coat the chicken in the seasoning, then roast it. Set aside to cool to room temperature, then pack into an airtight container.

Make the cheese and basil pull-apart and bake it after the chicken comes out of the oven. Wrap in a clean tea towel while still warm.

Coarsely shred the cucumber for the salad and store in a separate airtight container.

Heat the milk for the hot chocolate and pour into a thermos.

Just before serving

Toss the carrot, cucumber, dressing and hazelnuts together for the salad.

Dust the friands with icing sugar.

Pour the hot milk into cups and serve with the chocolate marshmallow skewers.

Cosy night in with friends

A winter chill in the air is as good a reason as any to spend the day indoors cooking up a sensational feast that will fill the house with warmth and tempting aromas. As your guests arrive, put another log on the fire, turn on some soft music and settle in for a long, relaxing, stress-free evening, sharing some wonderful comfort food.

Menu for 6

· · · · · · · · · · · · · · · · · · · ·

1 × Sesame prawn toasts (page 136)

1 × Red duck curry (page 23)
1 × Slow-cooked curry-crusted lamb with spiced rice (page 145)
1 × Lime & ginger marmalade glazed vegetables (page 116)

1 × Chocolate rhubarb waffle pudding (page 187)

3 × Hot chocolate mallow sticks (page 72)

Get organised

The day before

Complete steps 1 & 2 of the red duck curry recipe. Allow the coconut cream and spice mixture to cool, then store in airtight container in the fridge. Remove the duck meat from the bones and shred it, then refrigerate in an airtight container.

Cook the spiced rice and refrigerate in an airtight container.

Dip the marshmallows in chocolate and allow to set, then thread onto skewers, wrap in foil and refrigerate.

9 hours before guests arrive

Cook the slow-cooked curry-crusted lamb, remove from the oven and allow to stand in the pan, tightly covered with a lid.

Up to 4 hours before guests arrive

Process the prawn mixture for the prawn toast and refrigerate in an airtight container. Cut the bread into triangles.

Complete steps 1–4 of the chocolate rhubarb waffle pudding recipe, cover the puddings and allow to stand at room temperature. Don't preheat the oven.

Up to 1 hour before guests arrive

Remove the curry sauce and duck from the fridge to reach room temperature.

Prepare the lime & ginger marmalade glazed vegetables and cook them once the lamb comes out of the oven to rest.

30 minutes before serving main meal

Complete step 3 of the red duck curry recipe and cook the rice noodles.

Just before serving

Complete the preparation of the prawn toasts, then cook.

Cook the beans and warm spiced rice to go with the lamb.

Just before you sit down to the main meal, put the chocolate rhubarb waffle puddings into the oven.

Make the hot chocolates.

Acknowledgements

Publishing a cookbook requires time, patience, dedication, bucketloads of confidence in the author and a huge financial gamble on the part of the publishing house, and for all these things I thank Random House Australia and in particular, Nikki Christer, my publisher. To my editor, Elizabeth Cowell, thank you for your kind, gentle nature, attention to detail and understanding. Thanks also to the production team, especially Linda Watchorn, production manager, who worked tirelessly to get this book off to print, and to the sales and marketing teams who support and maintain the presence of my books in stores; to Emma Caddy, my publicist, a beautiful, patient, kind soul who loves talking and eating with me; and to Future Classic for another stunning design job.

Thanks to Alex and Kellie, my makeover team, who I love for the fab wardrobe, hair and make-up on the cover and in the images of me throughout the book; to Mel, my niece; and to Mark, Gail and the Walsh family for your generosity on a successful cover shoot.

Steve Brown – what can I say that I haven't said before about the photographer who has snapped every single image in this book? He is a genius and a gentleman, and the images are more beautiful than ever. Thank you for your generosity, creativity and all the coffee – I adore you.

Kate Nichols, a special friend and colleague. Thanks for cooking at the shoot, reading through all my recipes, working through the content and being a sounding board for everything in between – I look forward to the day I can return the favour on a book that carries your name.

To Shelley, the creator of Mud Ceramics, and her team, who allow me to wander through their warehouse picking up gorgeous pieces to use throughout my book; to Georgie at Major & Tom for the timeless old wares; and to Victoria at Village Living – your generosity is humbling.

To my family and dear friends, thank you for taste-testing, always being at the end of the phone, and sharing your love and life with me. I treasure the part you play in my life and know I am the person I am today because of you.

Janelle

Index

Available now
at all good bookstores

An Ebury Press book
Published by Random House Australia Pty Ltd
Level 3, 100 Pacific Highway, North Sydney NSW 2060
www.randomhouse.com.au

First published by Ebury Press in 2010

Addresses for companies within the Random House Group
can be found at www.randomhouse.com.au/offices

National Library of Australia
Cataloguing-in-Publication Entry

Bloom, Janelle.
Family food & weekend feasts / Janelle Bloom.

ISBN 978 1 86471 123 3 (pbk).
Cookery.
641.5

Cover and internal design by Future Classic
Printed and bound by Imago in China

10 9 8 7 6 5 4 3 2 1